BOTIJA

BOTIJA

A Shattered Identity Restored by Grace

Joanette C. Rodriguez

Hardcover: 978-1-951475-14-7
Paperback: 978-1-951475-00-0
eBook: 978-1-951475-01-7

Library of Congress Control Number: 2020924275

First paperback edition January 2021

Any references to historical events, real people, or real places are used fictitiously. Names, characters, and places are products of the author's imagination.

Edited by Avodah Editorial Services
Cover Art by Cody Silver
Layout by Cody Silver

Arrow Press Publishing
245 Pemberly Blvd
Summerville, SC 29486

www.arrowpresspublishing.com

Dedication

To my *abuelo*.

On March 15, 2020, my *abuelo* asked me during our telephone conversation if I still planned to pursue that "thing" we had formerly discussed, which I will disclose later in this book. I affirmed to him that the only reason why my cancer process was worth the fight was because if I had not pursued my dream, I could have lost my life and that my dream saved my life. With those words I said to him, he gave me his blessing and we prayed for healing and God's protection over my life and purpose. He also gave me this verse, and to be honest, I did not understand why: "After that, we who are still alive and are left will be caught up together with them in the clouds to meet the Lord in the air. And so we will be with the Lord forever. Therefore encourage one another with these words" (1 Thessalonians 4:17–18 NIV)

On June 15, 2020—the day we buried my grandfather, two days before my last round of chemotherapy—I accepted my reality. Praise the Lord for this day. My grandfather would no longer be far away in Puerto Rico, but he would be watching me from heaven instead. He now gives eternal glory to our Father. His passing restored the meaning of life for my family as we celebrated the surprises my grandfather left for us to unwrap during the days after his passing, the greatest gift being his legacy.

He served, led, mentored, advised, gave to, ministered to, challenged, and befriended many people. He transformed their lives in Jesus's name for the sake of the kingdom. My grandfather's trajectory reminds me of the alignment between past and present. He didn't hold back. He didn't complain. He didn't give up. He didn't resign. He didn't shut down. He didn't stop. He didn't trade his eternal salvation for anything this life tossed at him. Cancer, sickness, hurricanes, earthquakes, and famine did not deter him from serving his heavenly Father. My grandfather served with integrity, good moral character, discipline, tenacity, and, above all, love.

TABLE OF CONTENTS

Acknowledgments

Dear Friends,

Never would I have imagined the ink of my pen would press words of hope and faith during a new season defined by cancer, chemo, surgery, recovery, and survival. I am preparing for a series of events I thought were a dream or a mere figment of my imagination, until January 31, 2020 when Dorothy, my oncologist's nurse, called me and confirmed that I have breast cancer.

As I prepare for the greatest challenge I have yet to face, I say to you, I have faith, hope, joy, and trust in the Lord like never before. I am excited because He did not let me come into 2020 with vain imagination but an unclouded vision for what was to come: my process, the test, and clear instructions I must follow. I trust His Word, I love His Word, and I look forward to this journey.

Be strong and of good courage, do not fear nor be afraid of them; for the Lord your
God, He is the One who goes with you. He will not leave you nor forsake you.
Deuteronomy 31:6

I want to thank, in advance, everyone who has stood up and prayed in faith that God's will would be fulfilled in my life. I thank you for believing in me and encouraging me to be strong and steadfast. I thank God for my bosses at SEU, my colleagues, and my friends who have encouraged me to accept the proper medical plans, facilities, and coverage, but more for their fervent prayers when I began my first day of work on November 20, 2019.

Thank you for never giving me a hard time when I needed to take off to deal with logistics and planning for my treatment.

Thank you to my family at Segadores de Vida (SDV) in Southwest Ranches, Florida, for the prayers in faith that I would be healed and cured miraculously, for praying that I could be healed in the name of Jesus, for declaring the Word in my life, for hanging onto my faith through the journey of discovery and faith in Christ.

Thank you to The Potter's House Ministries in Dallas, Texas; Ministerio Centro Cristiano Soplo de Vida in Dominican Republic; Federacion CCN in Venezuela; Casa de Amor y Fe in Lakeland, Florida; El Trovador Javier Rodriguez in Puerto Rico; Montclair Tabernacle Church of God in Dumfries, Virginia; Apostle Franklin Susana-Gomez in Rotterdam, Netherlands; Iglesia de Dios Canaan in Woodbridge, Virginia; and all the appointed leaders and disciples of Christ who considered me when praying for a miracle.

For every high priest taken from among men is appointed or men in things pertaining to God, that he may offer both gift and sacrifices for sins. He can have compassion on those who are ignorant and going astray, since he himself is also beset by weakness. Because of this he is required as for the people so also for himself, to offer for sins. And no man takes this honor to himself, but he who is called by God, just as Aaron was.
Hebrews 5:1–4

Thank you, Mom, Dad, and Ismael, for being here at my side from the moment I knew what was to come. Thank you for listening, for comforting me, and for sharing time with me in the presence of the Holy Spirit as we fellowshipped through this process. Thank you for responding to my emotional needs for family and unity during a transitional period in our lives and for being present. Thank you to my brother for being here to listen and bond with me during a challenging time regardless of the obstacles and challenges you also faced. I praise God for His forgiveness and healing in our family.

Thank you to my grandmother, uncle, and aunt for coming along with me on the journey and for desiring the unity and fellowship despite the circumstances. Thank you to my extended family for responding with prayers and support, for your thoughts and genuine love through different avenues despite the distance and turmoil you were facing in Puerto Rico. No earthquake could shake your faith and hope. You remained so loving and kind in your words and thoughts toward my family, and I thank you.

The Lord bless you and keep you; the Lord make His face shine upon you, and be gracious to you; the Lord lift up His countenance upon you, and give you peace."
Numbers 6:24–26

Thank you to my sisters who were present and offered prayer and support despite the distance and sent me all the love through social media. Thank you to Titi Carmen, Pastora Yolanda, and Pastor Roubert for declaring the word of healing and provision, of love, and of truth into my life without ceasing. Thank you for never believing in the problem and maintaining hope and faith in the living Word of God for our future generations.

Let us hold fast the confession of our hope without wavering, for he who promised is faithful. Hebrews 10:23

Thank you, friends, for letting your hearts and spirit yield to the Lord and for accepting His love and faithfulness through the course of my process and for believing in His power, His grace, His favor, and His benevolence. Thank you for accepting this challenge as your opportunity to witness a glorious transformation that will increase your faith for which only He gets all the glory and honor.

Let us therefore be diligent to enter the rest, lest anyone fall after the same example of disobedience. For the word of God is living and powerful, and sharper than any two-edged sword, piercing even to the division of soul and spirit, and of joints and marrow, and is a discerner of the thoughts and intents of the heart. And there is no creature hidden from his sight, but all things are naked and open to the eyes of Him to whom we must give account.
Hebrews 4:11–13

I want to give God praise and thankfulness for my husband and son. Without knowing, believing, and hoping in faith that only God can carry me through this, it would be difficult to push forward. In God's sovereignty and grace,

I was blessed with our child and marriage, and genuine interest in God's kingdom and purpose. I thank God for the privilege to serve Him with my life and give this process my full intent to heal, survive, and testify for the rest of my days what His grace did for me in the name of Jesus Christ, my Savior, my redeemer, and my eternal Father.

Though one may be overpowered by another, two can withstand him.
And a threefold cord is not quickly broken.
Ecclesiastes 4:12

Introduction

What if, on the journey to self-discovery, we realize we are malleable clay in the hands of our creator?

Paul ponders, "Does not the potter have the right to make out of the same lump of clay some pottery for special purposes and some for common use?" (Romans 9:21 NIV). When we understand the process of the clay in the potter's hands, we discover the process we must all endure in becoming mature followers of Jesus chosen for a higher calling.

Clay can be harvested from riverbanks and creeks, or by digging in the ground in areas that have clay-rich soil. Sand and small stones mixed into the clay can give a different texture, and clay comes in many colors, from white to red to dark gray.

The importance of knowing and understanding who we are stems from choosing first whom we will serve. You may have heard the Scripture, "But if you refuse to serve the Lord, then choose today whom you will serve. Would you prefer the gods your ancestors served beyond the Euphrates? Or will it be the gods of the Amorites in whose land you now live? But as for me and my family, we will serve the Lord" (Joshua 24:15 NLT). When we have chosen whom we will serve, Christ our Lord and Savior, we no longer live in our old patterns and beliefs, hosting spirits of darkness but of light. When we choose to truly live by these fruits of the Spirit, we begin to discover our original identity and purpose in life. We will know the truth and the truth will set us free (see John 8:32).

Jesus Christ who has saved us by grace will return soon and take us up to meet our Father in heaven face-to-face. For this, my friends, we must be ready. We are constantly bombarded with vain thoughts about our identity through the influence of those raising us, teaching us, and inspiring us. Whether personally or superficially through social media platforms, we focus our attention on searching for meaning and purpose in life.

Paul also teaches us to be not conformed to the patterns of this world but to be transformed by the renewal of our mind (see Romans 12:2). In that same light, we are told by Jesus in Scripture that in this world we will face adversity but that we know whom to trust in, our Lord, because He has overcome the dark ruler of this world. In John 10:10, He says, "The thief's purpose is to steal and kill and destroy. My purpose is to give them a rich and satisfying life." By this Jesus is not referring to tangible riches or things, but the abundant life in which our soul prospers. When our soul prospers, everything prospers: our life, our health, our wealth, our family, our marriage, our businesses, and our assignments. Though we may wonder, But how? It happens as we change our minds and refocus all our faith and trust in the Lord.

Whether we have believed lies that have fed our heart, our soul, and our spirit, resulting in wayward thinking, stagnation, impotence, and apathy, these lies also steal our peace and our joy, kill our hope and faith, and eventually destroy our purpose and assignment in this world. We must learn how to let those things go through Christ so that we can be made whole again and prosper as a body in Christ. The good news is "you, dear children, are from God and have overcome them, because the one who is in you is greater than the one who is in the world" (1 John 4:4 NIV). This has been the revelation that I have received throughout my walk with the Lord Jesus Christ, and I couldn't wait to tell you all about it.

My hope for you is that this book will inspire you to seek God's wisdom every day and that you also choose to overcome fear with faith, forgive and be forgiven, experience breakthroughs, and develop endurance through your breakthrough healing process. Your need for healing may have stemmed from some form of mental, emotional, or spiritual sickness; a divorce; bankruptcy; or any form of physical or sexual abuse, but you will understand how to navigate your journey if you read the Word of God and embrace His everlasting grace in your life.

I encourage you to receive this testimony of restored faith, hope, and love from the words of this book inspired by the Holy Spirit. In it I detail my strategies such as prayers I wrote, Scriptures I read, and key speakers I listened to whom God used to help me renew my mind. As I walked this journey, I discovered along the way several full-circle moments experienced while pursuing God-given dreams. I realized God was not finished with me, and I can guarantee that, if you are reading this, He is not finished with you either.

All good pottery clay should be able to be tied in a knot. If the clay ties into a knot without breaking, it is usually a suitable candidate for pottery. Clay is often fresh and wet when harvested out of the ground, although in more arid climates, it is collected dry. When it is handpicked, rolled into a knot, wet, dried, rewet, formed, and fired, the result is a fine finished ceramic piece.

But when the fine ceramic piece breaks, it is customary to sweep up the pieces and dump them in the trash bin. Unless the potter decides these pieces can be re-collected from the floor, rewet, refired, reformed, refined, and refinished to perfection. That is what Potter we serve, a good God who will not throw away what He has masterfully crafted. For as King David wrote in Psalms 139:14, "I praise you because I am fearfully and wonderfully made; your works are wonderful, I know that full well."

We are clay in our creator's hands. Once we have realized we have a deep hunger and thirst for a relationship with God, we begin to discover our purpose in life. This refining process produces total dependence on Him, and we begin to comprehend how only He can fill our clay pot with eternal grace, hope, and joy by faith in Jesus.

SECTION ONE

Shaping the Clay

CHAPTER ONE

The Early Days

*Think back on those early days when you first learned about Christ. Remember how
you remained faithful even though it meant terrible suffering. Sometimes you were
exposed to public ridicule and were beaten, and sometimes you helped others who were
suffering the same things. You suffered along with those who were thrown into jail, and
when all you owned was taken from you, you accepted it with joy. You knew there were
better things waiting for you that will last forever. So do not throw away this confident
trust in the Lord. Remember the great reward it brings you! Patient endurance is what
you need now, so that you will continue to do God's will. Then you will receive all that
he has promised.*
Hebrews 10:32–36 NLT

Boty

      Our first identity is determined by our name. When I was young and people
asked my name, I would say, "My name is Joanette Cristina Rodriguez, but everyone
calls me Boty." My parents told me a Mexican family friend named me Botija from
the popular show "El Chespirito" because I was a fat baby. I didn't walk much as
a toddler, and I was often told that I loved to eat and sleep as a baby. Although my

older brother Ismael called me Boty because of the mispronunciation of Botija, for years others switched it up to Botiquin, Botiviri, Bots, Botilda, and Boty-La, among other nicknames. I signed my legal name "Boty" because I believed it was a part of me, and never questioned why my nickname was Boty until others asked what it meant.

When my husband told me he would call me only by my name, Joanette, I wondered if I would ever go by Boty again. Was it necessary to explain my name every time I met someone new, let alone the meaning? My husband asked me when we first became a couple, "Who are you?" I became frustrated because I did not know how to answer the question. It took some time, but eventually I began to realize the question I was being asked.

He also asked me if I believed in the Father, the Son, and the Holy Spirit. I then realized the questions didn't have anything to do with my name, where I came from, or what I did for a living. It was not about my background; it was about my spirituality. He could see that who I really was had been masked, as if I had taken on many different minds that weren't my own. I struggled with these questions as much as I struggled with my faith and Christianity being challenged by people in conversation and relationship.

A series of events the Holy Spirit brought to my memory during chemotherapy, despite brain fog, led me to write the story of my life while simultaneously experiencing a healing journey in pursuit of my dreams. This story depicts my life from the early stages of my youth through the teenage years, recounting the events which led to my then flawed but now renewed identity. Memories depicted in this book may resonate with you if you already know me (I have always been an open book), but most importantly, I want to share how each step in my healing from verbal abuse, emotional abuse, and eventually sexual abuse led to a total restoration in my spiritual, physical, and emotional health through faith.

For many years I believed these events represented who I was, until everything I ever thought represented me was shattered and was remade, revealing the true design of my identity through Christ. Second Corinthians 4:7 tells us, "But we have this treasure in jars of clay to show that this all-surpassing power is from God and not from us" (NIV). This verse helped me understand that no matter what details describe the story of my past and the effects on the exterior, I believed a new story would be written to reveal the treasures that represent who I am by faith, prayer, and revelation from the Word of God. Regardless of what the Enemy tried to do, I discovered the potential I had to either keep making a mess out of Boty, or to trust in God to lead me along the still waters and reveal His plans for my life.

Military Brat

Born to Puerto Rican parents in Clarksville, Tennessee, I was raised in a U.S. Army family in Germany. Shortly after arriving to Frankfurt, Germany, my family joined a Christian church. I enjoyed Sundays. I was three when I began singing with my father "Quiero estar contigo" (I Want to Be with You), "Mi Pensamiento Eres Tu Senor" (My Thoughts Are with You, Lord), and "Esta Lucecita" (This Little Light of Mine). I would sit with my father while he played his guitar, and practice vocals with him for Sunday worship. I would ask him for the microphone in Spanish, el tucrofono, and he would say, "it's not tucrofono, its microfono," translated to English, "your-crophone" versus "my-crophone."

My first childcare experience was with my German oma. My aunt Titi Carmen also came to live with us for some time in Germany, and she would also take care of my older brother and me. I enjoyed la choquera (the slide) at the park on the military housing installation and going to church with my parents. My dad was a soldier in the United States Army and my mom was a civilian secretary for the Department of Defense.

In 1989, around my fourth birthday, my mom, my brother Ismael, and I moved from Germany to Puerto Rico to live with my grandparents. My dad deployed to Kuwait during the Gulf War and we remained with my grandparents for one year. During that time of my life, I experienced a full cultural immersion in my Puerto Rican roots. I was quite the affectionate child and was earnestly sought by the elders of the church for my long hair and loving ways, so I've been told. I attended church with my grandparents at the Salvation Army of Ponce, Puerto

Rico, where my grandparents served loyally for over forty years.

I enjoyed taking naps with my abuelo, playing with my little cousin Normarie when she was just a baby, and going to the neighborhood limber stand (Puerto Rican frozen custard) for a twenty-five-cent limber. Mom would take my older brother Ismael to his school and I would spend the day with my grandmother who taught me songs, how to pray, and how to read the Bible. By the age of four, I could recite Psalm 121 in Spanish.

Narizona (Big Nose)

I was six years old when my father received his orders for Fort Bragg, North Carolina. My family moved there, and I began kindergarten the following school year. My first language was Spanish because it was our primary spoken language at home. Learning English began the first week of kindergarten in Fayetteville, North Carolina. My parents bought their first home in Raleigh, North Carolina, and shortly after that, my grandmother came to visit from Puerto Rico, then Titi Carmen and Normarie. We integrated into an English-speaking Church of God in Fayetteville.

I became a cheerleader for the children's church ministry "Sunshine Avenue," and my parents became more involved in the discipleship program for ministry training. I had a prayer mom whom I loved dearly, Sister Shelley Maldonado, and her daughter Stacey became like a sister to me. Within eighteen months, however, we received orders to return to Germany. Dad would leave first to prepare the way, then we would follow a few months later.

At first, we attended the English-speaking ministry sponsored by the Military Ministries and the Church of God, but by the time I was nine, we had begun attending the Hispanic ministry in Heidelberg. At the church meetings, I began making friends who lived on other military bases. I attempted to invite other Latinas to my church by placing invitation cards on their parents' car windshields. Mom always said that I was *tremenda* (daring).

As a child, I thought the greatest blessing of living overseas was when Titi Carmen and her family were also stationed in Germany and we were able to spend holidays together. It was a blessing to fly my grandparents from Puerto Rico to Europe and vacation with them. We took various trips to the theme parks in Germany and Holland, making lifelong memories. Unplanned excursions to historical places such as museums, castles, and parks were among the greatest memories my family shared while living in Europe.

Titi Carmen and her family lived a few hours away from us for four years. We would visit each other on the weekends and even go to church together. My cousin Normarie's and my favorite things to do were to play "church" and "restaurant."

Normarie was seven, I was eleven, and she would say to me, "I'll preach. You sing, Boty!" Our parents would hide behind the cracked door and watch us. We couldn't stay out of my aunt's bag of instruments, and those tambourines were always clanging as we pretended to speak in tongues and fall down in the Spirit. When we played restaurant, we mimicked what we saw our parents and other adults do. We would trade off being waiter and guest, starting off with, "Smoking or non-smoking?" because back then smoking inside public places was permissible.

When our parents' involvement in ministry intensified and conflict of interests arose between the adults in our lives, from parents, to pastors, and other church members, the separation in my family and dynamics were instinctively noticeable. We tried to come together a few times but there was always a resounding argument between our dads. During a family trip to Puerto Rico right after Titi Carmen and the family were given order to move to New York State, our dads were arguing in the street in front of my *abuelo's* house and I was holding my two-year-old cousin Tito. I had to hand Tito over to Titi Carmen and say my farewell until the next three years passed and we were able to meet again stateside.

When we returned to Germany, we experienced separation and great sorrow from that point forward. Titi Carmen had been a part of Ismael's and my lives for almost our entire childhood. I had even been the flower girl in her wedding. Normarie and Tito were my only cousins on my dad's side, and we could no longer spend holidays together as we once could. So many things were never clear, but I guessed they were not for me to understand. Titi Carmen's pastor had said to me,

"Walk away. This is an adult conversation," while talking to my uncle. I will never forget the moment I remember feeling *narizona* (big nose), and sensing issues in the atmosphere but later my mom told me that I was always inquisitive.

Not that I was nosey, but I was always involved in my parents' church affairs from an early age. My mom has told me that when I was born, she looked at my nose to see if it was big and then said, "Ruth Fernández." (Ruth was a famous singer, not that I mind being compared to an iconic figure from Puerto Rico.) It made me a bit self-conscious because I believed that I had a big nose and that made me feel ugly.

Mom was expressive but not affectionate. She would tell me things just as she thought them, and I suppose she did not realize I was incapable of processing what she meant to say or do when she was upset. I remember when I was nine years old and I picked up a rock outside and drew a heart on the microwave door. She was outraged. I wrote her an apology on an extra valentine's day card I had from school which I know she preserves in her Bible to this day.

Conceited

In the sixth grade, when I began middle school, I was often made fun of by the kids at school. They would call me names such as Mr. Ed because of my long dark ponytail and big white teeth, and they bullied me in the PE locker room and cafeteria just because they "didn't like" me. I got nicknames like "switcharoo" because I walked with a switch, and "stuck-up" because I appeared snobby to them. Mom was always correcting my posture when we took photos at the church. She would always say, "Straighten your back," because I had a slouching issue.

Frequently, church life carried over into the week, and on school days it was challenging to remain focused on my academic priorities. We had a robust schedule with church on Sundays, Tuesdays, Fridays, and some Saturdays, not to mention Sunday afternoon fellowship. Many of our conversations on our way to and from church were about the ministry, and church hurt.

It was not uncommon to talk about drama, attitudes, complaints, and routine challenges as we constantly spent time around other people with different goals and values, although we had some things in common (culture, religious beliefs, and the military). What was not common to talk about were age-appropriate subjects related to sexual immorality, faith, and implications of sin on the soul of man. Ambiguity and biblical illiteracy were already at the core of a mediocre spiritual formation. My mom always told me those topics were taboo when she was being raised, but she tried to talk to me about things she understood as they related to my physical development.

After my first kiss with my first boyfriend in the sixth grade, I was embarrassed and ran home because I had no idea what I was doing. That followed me through the end of my middle school years, and the boys would call me "frigid" because I did not kiss. I felt angry, and when they would pick on me, particularly one of them who I liked for a long time, I slapped him and got suspended for fighting in school on two occasions. I was developing a violent nature with boys, and I could not explain where it stemmed from. I never saw my mother behave in that manner. It could have been the mad women on the Spanish novellas (soap operas) I watched with mom. This was a turning point in my life, as I began to experience a desire to make friends and to be liked but people always had something to say about my attitude and my ways.

When I went to my friends' houses, I noticed something different about their family dynamics. I would notice that they were more down to earth, more loving, and more joyful. I thought it might be because of my parents' position at the church, but I did not understand the conflict and what was lacking in our home if it was love or too much discipline.

During my adult years, mom has shared with me about her struggles with people in the ministry, particularly while my dad was deployed, but when he would return home, how things would shift. Mom was caring and compassionate toward my brother and I and always took care of the entirety of things during dad's absence. She worked, she kept up with ministry, she cooked, trained during her lunch hour often at work, and devoted time to her studies at the University of Maryland, while assuming the role of disciplinarian when my brother and I misbehaved.

Once dad returned home, He would discipline us and set things in order in a more abrupt way but never withholding his explanation for why he was doing it. He wanted us to be upright and doing things as best as we were being raised up to, as Christian. At the time, post-traumatic stress disorder wasn't given a name. He had his good days and his rough days dealing with things as a soldier in the Army, with his schooling, military, and raising a family. My parents wore multiple hats and at various times, tried the best they could in my opinion.

Although one or two other families appeared to be loyal friends to my family, and Dad made a few good friends who to this day remain close with him, quite often I would hear about the things my mom was told by other women in ministry which later may have played a part marking our thought patterns for my future. Mom never believed some of the things she was told, nor did she repeat them to me as a child, but somehow, they left a lasting impression on how she felt about raising me up to prove others wrong. I believe the result of open ears and trust in the wrong individuals can provoke the wrong interpretation of who we are and plays a role in how we perceive the spirit of God.

Mom and Dad experienced deception, betrayal, and accusations that would cause pain and discomfort in trusting specific people in ministry on one hand, but on another, the inability to channel these feelings mixed with the perversion of sin, I feel that things were subtly introduced into our family to cause destruction. Although I was never too sure who, what, when, where, how, or why, Mom told me, she was told when I was just a child, *"Boty will grow up to be "exotic" and "a lesbian."*

I knew something didn't seem right each time we transitioned and eventually ended up attempting to have church in the living room of our apartment as a family. In my personal assessment of the situations, I was never going to become either of those, I simply did not understand the differences between curiosity and sexuality. At the time, she did not talk to me about these comments. She just taught me to be conservative, responsible, hardworking, and remain pure. I enjoyed mimicking her ways as a child and teenager, I wanted to play secretary with Mom's work supplies and house with my girlfriends from church. I didn't know what I wanted, but I certainly did not dream about prince charming or being daddy's little princess.

There was a distinction between who I was becoming and the reality of my household dynamic. Dad was always on a mission and very dedicated to things without an overwhelming expression of affection toward us. Dad and I exchanged letters during his time away from home and when he returned, he knew my fascination with VW's so he would always bring me a toy VW car, a piggy bank, or a stuffed animal to express his thoughtfulness.

My friends could cut and color their hair. They would ask me, "Why aren't you allowed, Boty?" I always had long hair, and my mom claimed it was "their jealousy and envy" that would prompt them to ask me that. She would also tell me, "That is the veil God gave you, and when you were a little girl, I promised Him I would never cut your hair." I also was not allowed to shave my legs, and they were hairy. My friends would tell me, "You really should shave your legs, Boty." I could do some things, but I couldn't push my luck with my mom when it came to her rules about my hair.

Mom let me use cosmetics around the age of eleven. I would use my friend's makeup at school, and my mom said, "If you're going to sneak it, I might as well buy you your own, so you don't catch an infection or something." I also liked playing dress-up and having pictures taken of myself. In those days, JCPenney's, Chadwick's, and Victoria's Secret were only available by catalogue. I would take Mom's catalogues and pretend to pose like the models in the pictures.

I was into modeling and really believed I could become Miss Universe someday. Then one day when I was in the ninth grade, my science teacher stopped me on my way out of her classroom. She said, "Joanette, your beauty won't get you anywhere."

I thought she was right. I was always getting in trouble for being chatty and looking at myself in a mirror. My favorite class in high school was cosmetology. I didn't enjoy reading, math, or science. I had always struggled with these subjects, having trouble with reading comprehension and being a poor test taker. I enjoyed talking about boys, beauty products, and novellas. I also enjoyed long walks with my best friend, Tania, and we had ongoing conversations about a crush or our next trip to Italy, France, or Belgium with the church youth group.

When I took a job at Popeye's in the military exchange food court, I ended up quitting shortly after because I refused to remove my acrylic nails. My friends called me conceited, but I thought it was normal to be girlie. I even ran like a girl, or so they said in PE classes throughout high school. If only I had known about Esther growing up. It would explain why I enjoyed looking in the mirror so often and my sudden inquisitive ways for seeking a meaning in life.

Before each young woman was taken to the king's bed, she was given the prescribed twelve months of beauty treatments—six months with oil of myrrh, followed by six months with special perfumes and ointments. When it was time for her to go to the king's palace, she was given her choice of whatever clothing or jewelry she wanted to take from the harem. That evening she was taken to the king's private rooms, and the next morning she was brought to the second harem, where the king's wives lived. There she would be under the care of Shaashgaz, the king's eunuch in charge of the concubines. She would never go to the king again unless he had especially enjoyed her and requested her by name.

Esther 2:12–18 NLT

Bocona (Big Mouth), *Mandona* (Bossy), and *Sangana* (Wimp)

My biggest challenge in grade school was keeping quiet. I was very talkative. I didn't consider myself timid or shy. In fact, most of the time, I would pursue friendships with people if I felt a connection to them by asking them a simple question: "Do you speak Spanish?"

Sometimes I would initiate small talk with a compliment or a smile. In eighth grade I won "Best Smile" at my prom, which I wasn't allowed to attend due to the required Friday night church service. Though I became known for my smile, my parents had other ideas for me.

My mom told me I would be a leader, while my dad claimed I was too opinionated. He would often say, "What happens in this house stays in this house," and he would warn me, "Don't talk." Mom, on the other hand, compared me to other family members and would say, "You are bocona" (big mouth), because the projection and tone of my voice reminded her of them. I was always fascinated with the diary of Anne Frank and watching the films depicting her story during

WWII, particularly when Peter refers to her as "Ms. Quack Quack" because she talked a lot in school. One day her teacher asked her to write a story and she wrote: A Story by Anna Frank, the tale of a duck family and a black swan to read it out loud in her class. I could relate with her behaviors in the history books and perhaps that's the reason why Mom always gifted me with journals and diaries, so that I could write

my own diary one day.

I knew I was bossy, and my brother nicknamed me Jezebel. I wasn't sure if it was because of my vanity or just because he felt as if I was trying to control him. Whenever he or I would get into trouble with our friends, my parents quickly fixated their eyes on the people we were hanging around. Little did they know, at an age where hormonal changes are ramped and curiosity is at peak, with Dad deployed constantly and mom working full-time, it was quite easy to get away with doing stereotypical "preacher's kid" shenanigans, being mischievous, and exploring our limits.

When we were not misbehaving, it was assumed that we were. My friends always said, "Boty, you are like a little adult. Your parents are so strict with you and Ismael." I believe the way my parents handled their discipline toward my brother and me played a role in my lack of trust and ability to make sound decisions for myself. Most of the time, decision making was out of fear of getting in trouble, being hit, or being embarrassed.

It made me feel like I couldn't really say what I wanted to say, and it was best to keep my mouth shut or else I would provoke my dad to anger. Similar to confessing your sins, it can be a scary step when you are told you will go to hell because you are treated as a menace to society. Anger and argument were common traits in my house growing up and they were mostly expressed through yelling, slamming, and hitting. I thought this was normal and accepted this form of expression until I was labeled "*bocona*."

My brother and I are three years apart. Mom always told me, "Ismael didn't want you to come when he knew I was pregnant with you," but then she would say, "He was always with you, Boty." These were the words I heard most of the time, although based on the family photos I prefer to describe a different version. We have always been conditionally amicable. We grew up close and spent time with each other through the good, the bad, and the ugly.

Sharing a typical sibling relationship, we fought, made up, and then got in trouble, and discipline was distributed equally by our parents. I never agreed to being punished publicly around my friends. Growing up in church, it was normal to step outside to be disciplined for misbehavior, but when I was fourteen, our church members took a coach bus trip to Rome, Italy. My brother got lost in the Vatican for about three hours, and everyone went into panic mode looking for him.

Later that afternoon, I suffered the ridicule from my dad when he hit me in front of all my church friends for walking off to a vendor's table. I guess he was nervous and didn't know how else to react. My mom's motto was always "50/50," and she made a conscious effort to treat us equally. She would take care of both of us and make sure we learned things like chores, cooking, and study habits from her.

My brother and I play fought often until it would get out of line and I got my feelings hurt, then my dad would say, "Don't be *sangana*" (a wimp). The truth is, he was just jumping on my case if he thought I was whining and that aggravated him. My brother and I were decently close until we got into typical sibling disputes and threatened to tell mom or dad what one of us had done mischievously. It was always easier to cover my brother's tracks than telling him I was going to snitch on him. Otherwise, he would call me an instigator. I discovered that although I knew right from wrong, if I would say it, I might come off as self-righteous, judgmental, and critical. Those were the names he would give me until our adult years when we had altercated arguments about each other's life choices concerning who we date, marry, or what we chose to do with our life outside of a Christian light. One moment we would trust each other and confess our sins to each other, the next moment we would become indifferent toward each other if we noticed a slip back into a self-harming behavior like a bad choice in relationship or conduct. In all our attempts to maintain a healthy relationship with boundaries, respecting each other's life choices and decisions, we struggled with the reality of painstaking consequences and how they would often bring separation.

How can you say to your brother, 'Brother, let me take the speck out of your eye,' when you yourself fail to see the plank in your own eye? You hypocrite, first take the plank out of your eye, and then you will see clearly to remove the speck from your brother's eye."

Luke 6:42 NIV

CHAPTER TWO

Preacher's Kid (PK)

Train up a child in the way he should go, and when he is old he will not depart from it.
Proverbs 22:6

Misionera (**Missionary**)

In 2000, before my family left Germany on military orders to Northern Virginia, I received a word from a visiting troubadour from Puerto Rico whom my pastors at the time esteemed greatly, Javier Rodriguez El Trovador. When he began playing his poetic songs on his guitar, he began to pray and prophesy over many of us who went to the altar for prayer. When he came to me, he placed his hand on my braided-bun and in his song, prophesied that I would be a missionary.

I'll never forget the moment I knew that I would follow that path. Of course, I would spend the rest of my days traveling the world and spreading the gospel, or at least that was what I thought a missionary represented. By this time, we had been rejoined to our church in Heidelberg, and part of our mission was to visit Hispanic ministries throughout Germany, Belgium, and Holland. My eyes began to see the greater need in this world for outreach and love. At the time, prostitution was legal in Holland and my parents were going into Amsterdam to witness and evangelize. For the first time I learned about poverty and need because I was being exposed to other socio-demographics and their needs. I understood the mission was greater than the places I had known.

Every time we went to Holland and visited our Dominican friend Franklin and his family, I would leave incredibly sad. Not only because I had a special fascination for the historical landmarks we frequented, but because the fellowship with this family made me feel welcomed branded my heart with an impression of charisma and love. The same effect would happen when they would visit us in Germany. I was fond of their ministry, their passion in worship and preaching of the gospel. I wanted to continue traveling, experiencing relationship with God and church friends, meeting new people, and participating in ministry, but what I didn't understand was the difference between a vision, a mission, a dream, a prophecy, a calling, a promise, a purpose, destiny, and a process, let alone a testimony. The only thing I knew was church, fear of going to hell, and how I should walk, talk, and dress to preserve my Christian reputation. At fourteen, all I could really focus on was leaving my childhood in Europe and moving to America, the land of the free.

Quinceañera

It was a year of transition—from one continent to another, one school to another, and one circle of friends to another. My mother decided it would be a great idea to gift me with a trip to my grandparents' home in Puerto Rico. Mom did not want me to stay alone at home as her and Dad worked almost two hours away from home and my brother was taking summer courses. I was excited to spend a month with my cousin and grandparents, but mostly I wanted to experience the vain ideas I had about being Puerto Rican. I looked forward to the rich cultural awareness, the food, the music, the weather, and the possibility of finding love.

While I was there, my days were highlighted by a summer crush. Mom was okay with my friendship with this fellow. She had known his mom in her youthful days of growing up in Puerto Rico, and his grandmother and aunt were very fond of my mother and me. On the other hand, my grandmother and uncle were not happy about his interest in me. Although he was permitted to come by and see me—often with an eight-foot fence separating us and under my grandmother's watch—we got to know each other and spent the summer talking on the phone and exchanging letters.

Shortly after I returned to Virginia, the United States was hit with the 9/11 attacks and I stopped hearing from him, only to learn later that he was deterred from pursuing anything further as he felt rejected by my grandparents. Later, when I was in college, he told me that the distance was a major factor, but the reality was he could not stand the rejection and that what kept us apart was my family. I wasn't accustomed to dating and being allowed to have a "boyfriend," so a long-distance relationship was not favorable at that age. Everything that happened during the month we would celebrate my *Quinceañera* and my brother Ismael's eighteenth birthday was overshadowed by 9/11.

Teach us to realize the brevity of life,
so that we may grow in wisdom.
Psalm 90:12 NLT

"PK" (Pastor's Kid)

As my interest in travel, international relations, student involvement, and cultural diversity grew, I became more involved in student organizations and the church my parents planted in Woodbridge, Virginia, in 2002. I trusted God's path was already set for me and I would stick to it. I began co-leading devotional worship and evangelizing activities with our co-pastor and his daughters. Our objective was to invite others to come to church and experience a new light on things our high school friends were not familiar with in their homes. I was named president of the youth group and began leading in-home cell groups and reaching the community and my school friends with persistence. As a teenager I was fortunate, as my mom was successful at getting my brother and I plugged into the Department of Defense every summer. I aspired to becoming a foreign affairs officer, an ambassador, the first female president of the United States, or an officer in the U.S. Armed Forces one day.

One of my greatest strengths was my ability to converse with professionals, and the discipline of working for the government at such a young age was beneficial. I was sixteen commuting with my mom and my brother to work at the Navy Annex in Arlington, Virginia. Eating lunch with my mom across the street at the Pentagon, taking strolls into the courtyard, talking, and meeting her coworkers and friends were some of the highlights from my summers as a teenager. She was working inside the exact corridor that was rebuilt post 9/11.

Life in ministry was jam-packed with planning events. I would dream about conferences, evangelizing, planning crusades, and speaking to large crowds. By the tenth grade I met a nice guy at school from Venezuela. My biggest desire was to see my high school boyfriend join me in church and come to the feet of Jesus Christ. Some of my fondest memories were at summer and winter youth retreats in Allentown, Pennsylvania, as discipleship and weekend revivals were refreshing to my spirit and heart.

While work and school were well balanced with church and my social life, I still faced the emotional challenges of sadness, disappointment, and heartbreak because of yet another romantic disillusion my junior year in high school. One day, I called my mom from the school administration office shortly after she had dropped me off and asked her to come and pick me up. I felt devastated because I saw the guy, I wanted to maintain a relationship with and the reality for us not being supported by my mom to date really made me sad. I wanted to go home, crawl in bed, and weep.

She picked me up, and on our way home she exclaimed that I needed to get it together. In other words, none of what had happened warranted so much drama and I was not able to channel my feelings appropriately. Her words struck me as hurtful, and I felt helpless in that area, but I also understood she did not want to see me sad over a boy. Mom told me she was not familiar with these matters because she had not dated, and my dad had been her only true boyfriend.

I wrote her a letter but never gave it to her. I always wished I would have. The letter expressed my feelings, my cry out for her to listen to my version of the story, and what my intentions were in having this relationship.

All roads don't lead to heaven. At seventeen, I experienced heartbreak when Oscar said to me, "We're like two parallel lines that could never cross." I struggled with my desire to have a relationship and remain a good Christian young lady all at once. I knew that dating and being a Christian were possible, because I had heard stories from my friends in church. I attempted to express this to my mom on several occasions, and to this day I still have the letter that I wrote her when my Oscar was sensing that we were breaking up due to her disapproval. He was a nice guy, he respected me, and he mostly enjoyed coming over and attempting to converse with my parents. On one occasion he expressed his intentions to continue dating after high school.

He expressed love through gifts, letters, and romantic dinners, and we dreamed about traveling to Europe one day because he had family in Spain. He was a great friend with lasting intentions until one day, our religious values could no longer mix. He had come from a Jehovah's Witness background and, well, I was the Christian pastor's daughter. This was more than a romantic disillusion, and I was discouraged and lacking hope. Had I become a religious girl, a hypocrite, a product of my own sins, or just the result of my upbringing? I wondered, if I had given mom this letter and she had read it, if things would have been different.

A Letter to My Mom:

Mami,

I know it is kind of awkward for me to be writing you a letter instead of talking to you but if I don't write then I may leave something out that I really would like for you to understand. I am in a difficult situation and I never knew it until now. To be honest with you I didn't know that having strong feelings for a person would lead to this. It may seem weird or pitiful to you but if I don't let you know then there is no point in expecting any positive results back. To be honest with you, I met Oscar and he taught me a lot of things. I know that like every high school couple we had our ups and downs, but the truth is that we learn from each other and grew in many ways. I have always been the type of person that no matter what the situation

I find myself in I always hide it and show my happy side.

You may think that I forgot everything and that I've learned to accept the fact that we can't be together anymore but no. I haven't. I know that it is wrong for me to be with a person that isn't Christian or "not our belief," but let's look at it this way, we are happy together as friends, together without doing bad things, going to the movies, to the malls, him coming over, going out with other friends, etc. But to me a friend isn't someone I conversate with in school, it's a person I can count on anytime.

Now, you and Papi have rapidly taken that privilege away from me for your reasons and I understand but if Papi has said that he feels bad for Oscar and you've said you have nothing against him, then what makes you think that he will feel loved or cared for if you guys have practically taken from us the only thing we have, a little trust and faith. This has nothing to do with church anymore because we cannot say we've helped him in that aspect. I've always said that I cannot do anything without your support and that is why I am unhappy. It's so hard for me to be happy and to make you and him happy because as soon as I feel like I'm having fun the right way I remember that you don't think the same way.

What do you think is best for me? To leave it at that and know that I care for him and I cannot be with him and be sad or wait until he leaves and let there be peace between all of us. I mean mom, it's easy for you to say it's wrong and to let go but it's hard for me to accept that I need to let go for you and that I love him and can't have your support or trust from you guys. Can you think about how I feel? He is in my school and I see him every day and why should I have to give up on a person that hasn't caused me harm? It's not puppy love, its true friendship. He is a friend who respects me. Do you honestly think that just because he doesn't go to our church and he is a male that makes him an evil person? I would be happier knowing that I can do things with your support and trust than behind your back.

I have prayed, I have given myself time and space, but I know that no matter how hard I try I will suffer. Mom, please don't make me choose. Just give me a chance to prove to you that our friendship is pure and honest, that I will not make bad choices, that we will help each other and that the way I feel for him is worth it.

Give me the chance. Mom you don't know how many nights I have prayed and cried and it's not easy. Every time I think about letting go of something so special and positive in my life, I feel a knot in my throat that just makes me want to cry. Every time you give me that look or mention him and all the sudden change your attitude towards him, it makes me feel like you're not doing this because God told you to but because you just don't want to accept that I am happy with him. If I didn't care about him it wouldn't be this hard for me. If he didn't respect me or at least have the same morals as me, it wouldn't be this hard. Mami, just give me the opportunity to be happy and let me prove to God that I am strong, and I can resist anything the devil tries to put in my way. Give me the chance to use the victory God gave me in every way. Let me have faith and pray. Just let me prove that to you.

You don't know how hard it has been to write this letter. I don't know how your response will be, but I'm just going to let you know now, Oscar's family is leaving to Spain, and he will be alone here for a year. He needs a family. I want to be there for him. Instead of judging or giving up, I want to help and just being a school companion isn't a friend. I want you guys to open the doors of our house to him whenever he feels sad or lonely. I am not asking you to let him sleep here. Look at the positive and accept him. Help me show him and care for him like no one else would do outside.

> *"And I will cause hostility between you and the woman,*
> *and between your offspring and her offspring.*
> *He will strike your head,*
> *and you will strike his heel."*
> *Genesis 3:15 NLT*

Pegajosa (Affectionate)

I was quite inquisitive all my childhood and well into my teen years. I was involved in adult affairs, always meddling, and seeking affection from those around me. Something just didn't click for me until later, when I realized how this could backfire and inevitably take me down a path of sorrow and pain. But we often overlook those warning signs because we are so reluctant to see our own sin, knowing that since the beginning God has spoken and given clear instruction.

I must have been warned by God and my parents, because unlike other people who chose a path of rebellion for their reasons, I was choosing mine out of the false belief in the words of a trusted person who said to me, "no one will know," "only you, me, and God," and "it would only be something you do with me." As if God was okay with this. I was naïve, immature, and vulnerable enough to listen to the clever serpent's whispers, just as Eve did in the garden of Eden.

Above all else, guard your affections. For they influence everything else in your life.
Proverbs 4:23 TLB

Meanwhile, my parents were pastoring the church, I continued to serve and support in the ministry, and we were crossing paths with many other Christian artists, evangelists, and influential ministers. As the time came for our church to celebrate our first, second, and third anniversary, a series of events took place which left a lasting impression on my perspective of ministry, integrity, and the hope for a future in ministry. Betrayal and conflict between families provoked by dysfunction and the lack of awareness of hidden sin in the church, and the shame I felt, was all it took for me to resign from ministry. I had become the biggest hypocrite I knew. I was full of shame, guilt, and sin in my heart. Adam and Eve knew this shame and guilt, as they would hide when they heard God's voice calling on them. I became afraid and an accomplice to wrongdoing.

My inability to express what I needed and what was happening to me was confusing. This lack of awareness and understanding in my emotions became a gateway for roots of bitterness, anger, hate, and addiction in my soul. I placed all of my hope into relationships with the wrong people. I no longer knew who or what to believe. I only wanted to be loved, accepted. My mom told me, "You've always been like this, *pegajosa* (clingy)."

When I attempted to speak to my dad and started a phrase with, "My friend said," he would interrupt me and say, "You don't have friends, you just know people." He had no idea that I had placed my trust in people from the church more than I should have.

Oscar had warned me that a day would come when I would know betrayal from within the Christian community. It was that same week he told me those words, we officially broke up, and the perpetrator of that scenario—the Enemy—was already waiting for me to fall into a trap. I was persuaded by his friendly gestures, his kind words, and the seductive method he tempted me with. The confusion of a secret relationship with a man fueled by emotions of longing to give and receive love, affection, and the illusion that one day this could end in a happily ever after setting versus the inevitable outcome of pain, addiction, bitterness, resentment, and overall emotional trauma.

The result of sharing my feelings of sadness from the break up with my high school boyfriend transformed into an encounter with someone of the Christian faith in whom I could talk to and would listen, someone who I admired and cared for deeply. I fell into a comfort zone with inappropriate forms of embrace I was longing for, only to discover a light form of affection such as a kiss, could result in disruptive thoughts of what it could be like to give myself completely to someone asking for my trust who was significantly older and wiser than my seventeen years of immaturity could refrain from accepting. Though in my opinion, I was old enough to give consent, it was unknown to me the gravity of this behavior and how it could be perceived by the legal courts today. I was a victim of my own emotional ignorance and his ability to manipulate me without even conceiving the notion that my outlook on marriage, family, and ministry would change forever.

This is what the Lord says:
"Cursed are those who put their trust in mere humans,
who rely on human strength
and turn their hearts away from the Lord.
Jeremiah 17:5 NLT

Jezebel

Rather than learning to say no when I knew something was wrong, I was becoming more passive toward my own rebellious behaviors with angry outbursts, vocalizing my indifference, and flirting with sin. Had I become exactly who people told my mom I would become? Had I become the Jezebel my brother called me? Who was I becoming?

I would express to anyone who brought up the subject of love or marriage that I would never get married, let alone have children. I could not see myself as a mother or wife, and I felt free to say those things. I lacked spiritual awareness and understanding of when this all began and how it had gone as far as it did. At this point, I did not recall the words *generational curse*, and certainly not *redemption*, *grace*, or *reconciliation*. I only knew that if someone found out the truth, I was doomed.

When I turned eighteen, a friend from church introduced me to a new guy, and he and I began dating. My parents gave us their approval, probably because he agreed to attend church with me. I will never forget when he said, "I want us to be like your parents when we get older." For the first time in my life I felt like I came from a normal family. I decided to attempt the "right path"—to stay in church and on a Christian path. I never wanted to confess everything I had done in secret to my parents, my boyfriend, my brother, or close friends from the church because of fear.

I had yet to discover how to identify the root of my emotional challenges and how they evolved into behaviors displaying rebellion. This would be a key to recognizing my need to repent and experience deliverance. But how do we do this when the root stems from verbal, emotional abuse, or even sexual abuse? God's desire is for us to be saved no matter how dark that valley of sin may have become. Before I graduated high school, I attempted to weigh my options between seminary, beauty school, and the local community college, without the slightest clue on what I would study. Although I aspired to go to college, it seemed a bit out of my league from an academic perspective and I felt intimidated because of my SAT scores.

Then on Thanksgiving night in 2003, as we gathered at a church friend's home, their son's girlfriend told me about her wonderful experience at Mary Baldwin College (MBC) and encouraged me to apply there. Karina, who is also Latina, expressed that the college had a greater desire for diversity and inclusivity. After I applied, I was pursued with persistence and admitted. Inspired and driven by the desire to explore my identity as a young woman, I chose to attend the private residential college for women in Staunton, Virginia—home of the fighting squirrels.

Listen to your father, who gave you life,
and don't despise your mother when she is old.
Get the truth and never sell it;
also get wisdom, discipline, and good judgment.
The father of godly children has cause for joy.
What a pleasure to have children who are wise.
So give your father and mother joy!
May she who gave you birth be happy.
Proverbs 23:22–25 NLT

CHAPTER THREE

Boldly Baldwin

The heavens are shocked at such a thing and shrink back in horror and dismay. For my people have done two evil things: They have forsaken me, the Fountain of living waters; and they have built for themselves broken cisterns that can't hold water! Why has Israel become a nation of slaves? Why is she captured and led far away?
Jeremiah 2:12–14 TLB

Fighting Squirrel

MBC was different from The Pentecostal Biblical Institute of Puerto Rico, which I had applied, been accepted to, and forfeited due to a sudden change of mind and discouragement. In its earlier years of establishment, though not religiously affiliated, MBC was known as the Augusta Seminary for Women. I was captivated by the Shenandoah Valley, the hills, the ladies who would become my sisters, and all the opportunities to lead. I was also thrilled about being two hours away from home. It was easy to transition into community living and balance the responsibilities of class, homework, and student organizations, because, due to my military upbringing, I had an innate ability to adapt to new environments on a moment's notice.

On the other hand, one thing that I found most challenging and felt inadequately prepared for were the 2004 elections and the social and political differences that surrounded me as I was not accustomed to dwelling among people outside of my socio-demographics and religious beliefs. Awkwardly enough, I knew what position I stood for on topics I had little to no understanding about (for example, women's rights, abortion, and sexual orientation), but now I was challenged with questions and thought patterns I had never given thought to. It was the first time in my life that I questioned my orientation, my thought process, how I felt about the subject matter, and what position I would adopt.

Common terms were tossed at me such as LUG (lesbian until graduation) or LGBT, and I was challenged with ideologies that I had thus far been taught were sin. It was my personal challenge that kept me from identifying the truth because I was sensitive to what others said and felt, but I lacked a true revelation about these matters. My identity at school was different than my identity at home. At home I was more authentic to my upbringing. At school I was intimidated by my own lack of biblical worldview.

Gullible

On March 14, 2005, I submitted an essay to my English Composition professor titled "Coming to Mary Baldwin College." In this essay, I expressed the differences in my lifestyle, my culture, and my community when compared to MBC. I wrote, "I remember my dad telling me, 'When you go to college you are going to experience many new situations, but just remember how we raised you. Some girls will go one way and some another way; now we will see how loyal you will be to the teaching we instilled in you.'"

During the first few weeks of college, I knew what those things would be. I felt as if I had coped well with the changes, but I also believed limitations would arise in the ways I spoke with people about God and the Bible. I was compromising my beliefs when they insisted on telling me how they felt. I had to learn to shut up and listen. I thought it was almost impossible to talk to my colleagues because they did not want to listen to me, and I did not want to hear what they had to say either.

On occasions when I spoke with my roommates about how I felt about an issue, we would end up having a huge dispute. After attending a diversity workshop my first weeks in college, I learn a lot about sexual orientation and learned to share with everyone despite our differences.

'Suppose someone secretly entices you—even your brother, your son or daughter, your beloved wife, or your closest friend—and says, 'Let us go worship other gods'—gods that neither you nor your ancestors have known. They might suggest that you worship the gods of peoples who live nearby or who come from the ends of the earth. But do not give in or listen. Have no pity, and do not spare or protect them."
Deuteronomy 13:6–8 NLT

While I was still new at MBC, an encounter with a friend changed my mind about how to develop friendships. I had to learn to be friendly no matter how people felt about me. I wanted to change people and make changes on campus. I learned that I was going down the wrong path if I set myself of for that task. I decided to keep my beliefs to myself. I did not understand this was a controlling behavior proving to be ineffective in my intent be a witness to others.

A friend told me that on first impression I came off as arrogant, and that I could not go around trying to change everyone. I told her that I was doing what I felt was right. She said I was not wrong, but that I would come off as judgmental and as the one who needed to compromise and respect other people's beliefs. I was already used to that position with my family, so I began to question my understanding of what was right. I made it my priority to learn how to develop those relationships more than my relationship with God.

Eventually, I was not able to express my true values because I questioned my own sexuality. I was no longer sure if I was a Republican or a Democrat, and I didn't understand why being able to choose if abortions were right or wrong mattered, particularly because of the arguments of "this is my body" or "what if I was raped?" I didn't know the difference between one or the other political parties from a thorough perspective. The fact that I lived in Germany for a larger portion of my childhood also resonated with me and I was more particularly drawn to what I understood to be socialism and communism from our travels and meeting people from Cuba and Czech Republic. I would learn more about the liberties of being an American in matters of healthcare, birth control, Plan B and "safe sex" tied into all these pro-choice methodologies in my conversations with classmates and friends in college. Rather than arguing my point or my belief, I empathized and embraced these moments of conversation and relief with the mixture of alcohol and loose language.

At the end of my freshmen year in college, I broke up with my boyfriend after dating for one year. He had given me a promise ring and I was attempting to uphold a relationship with him, but I had become less interested in dating and more into my social life at school. I told him that I didn't want to get married right after college anyway. I wanted to travel and live a carefree life.

When I explained to my mom I didn't want to get married or have children, she said, "Don't say that, because gay runs in the family." She then agreed with me when I said, "Well, if it wasn't for being a Christian, I probably would have wound up being that way anyway."

My friends at school became more like the family I wanted to have, the one that would listen without judgment, the one that would accept my flaws, and the one that would approve of my choices. I was determined to keep an open mind and preserve my friendship with women of all colors, sexual orientations, and beliefs. As I listened to my friends tell me about their unfortunate sexual traumatic experiences, it dawned on me for the first time that my outlook on my experience during high school was not that of a love affair like the novellas I loved to watch but that I had been a victim of statutory rape. It was the first time I realized I had been a victim in my own home where I believed I was safe. I discovered that at sixteen I was not in a secret relationship with a significantly older individual but that I had taken advantage of by my naivety and gullible nature. He seduced me into an affair taking away the last strand of innocence, my virginity well before God's perfect appointed time. Tears flowed down my face, but the comfort from other friends in my college dorm and a heavy load lifted from confiding in other young women with such a deep secret relieved me from the burden of feeling ashamed around them. But in my alone time, it was usually a different sense of burden.

Home for Summer

Over the summers, and on holiday weekends and special occasions, I would go home, but the most devastating heartbreaks came with those trips. I would end up in emotional, high-strung arguments with my mom about anything ranging from—dirty dishes, curfew, or just her questioning my behavioral habits. I began experiencing confusing thoughts and making sinful spur-of-the-moment decisions with my friends. During my time alone in my bedroom, I would write.

My Prayer Journal: May 24, 2005

Dear God,

Today I meditated on you and the desires of my heart. First and foremost, I desire to seek more of you and that you fill me with your presence and your love. Up until today, you have been faithful. I cannot say the same thing about myself, and if I do not tell you that, you already know it because you know what my heart feels, what my flesh desires, and what my mind thinks. I pray and ask that you save me and that you guide me the way you have throughout my whole life.

Lord, you know what I feel. You know who I am. At this point, the only thing I want to do is run into your arms and cry, but I feel like a coward. I feel too far away from you. I need you to pull me close and let me know how much you love me. I need to feel that you are there and that what I desire does not compare to the blessing you have for me, but how? How do I know?

I just wonder, Lord, have my decisions been correct? Am I selfish? Am I wrong for feeling the way I do? For a long time, I doubted my relationship with him (another guy at church), and now, Lord, I just feel very happy. I feel free. I just want and need one thing to feel better. I want you, and I know I need you and your forgiveness for all my actions, for my thoughts and for those feelings that have been distracting me from you.

Now I ask you, Lord, clean my mind. This guy, I've had a crush on him since the first day I met him, and I don't have to say his name because you know who he is. Lord, is what I feel right or wrong? Before anything continues, tell me things are happening for a reason. Tell me that what I feel is okay and that you got it all under control. I like him a lot, his personality, his sense of humor. He listens, and he's God fearing. Not to mention he's attractive.

Tell me, Lord. You know what's best for me. Just speak to me. I just ask you to look at my life and speak to me. I need to hear from you. Amen.

Acknowledge Him in all your ways and He shall direct your paths.
Proverbs 3:6

Remorseful

I spent time contemplating whether or not I should tell my mom about my sexual sin and experiences during my senior year in high school with that person whom she and dad had esteemed so dearly and how I slipped right into a whirlwind of sin, but I was afraid of what my parents would say or do. Instead, I journaled and waited for the opportune moment. I wanted to live a transparent life with my parents, but I was afraid they would judge me, they wouldn't understand, and they would rebuke me. I would tell my friends, "My mom couldn't handle the truth because she was so perfect growing up, according to her track record." No matter what I did, I felt criticized and misjudged. We would watch how other people would raise scandal and expose other people's sin from pulpits and public platforms and as I heard people ridicule, judge, or condemn others, I feared the worse things happening to other families, ministries, and people, if I exposed my own secrets. I was afraid that my parents would not know what to do and worse, what my brother would do, after all, he was my older brother and proved to me he did not like anyone getting close to me in a romantic manner.

I tried to spend as much time as I could with my friends Patty and Marissa from high school. Patty was one of my only high school friends who I stayed in touch with when I was away at college. At this point, my parents had just stepped down from pastoring the church in Woodbridge, Virginia, shortly before Dad's retirement from the Army. I didn't care too much about the details of what had occurred. I was used to moving from one house to another, from one church to another, and from one city to another. Patty was my friend through all the moves. Just like during my high school days, I enjoyed shopping, cosmetics, talking about a crush, and traveling. My new friends from MBC were always planning something different, like mixers (dances) and Christian outreach on campus. Many of us were PKs, and we would go to each other's churches on our travels to each other's hometowns.

What was uncommon for me was praying over meals with alcohol on the table and attending weekend revivals followed by late-night outings to the local bars and nightclubs. I knew that it was wrong, and like I should choose between one way of life or the other because of my convictions. But I struggled with the same desires as other college students. I slowly became more careless about the temptations, and little by little sin became more appealing. From roommate drama and boy troubles, to partying on holidays I had never celebrated during my upbringing, to all-nighters attempting to halfway finish my studies and maintain average grades, I was lost in a dark world void of Christ. But in my prayer journal, I would plead for God to rescue me out of my sin.

Israel failed to destroy the nations in the land, as the Lord had commanded them.
Instead, they mingled among the pagans and adopted their evil customs.
They worshiped their idols, which led to their downfall.
They even sacrificed their sons and their daughters to the demons.
They shed innocent blood, the blood of their sons and daughters.
By sacrificing them to the idols of Canaan, they polluted the land with murder.
They defiled themselves by their evil deeds and their love of idols was adultery in
the Lord's sight.
Psalms 106:34–39 NLT

My Prayer Journal: June 10, 2005

Dear God,

I know I have made the worst mistakes of my life. I want to ask you for forgiveness, Lord. I pray and ask that you examine my actions, and I plead that you have mercy on my life just one more time. I know you forgive and know you love me, because you have sent your son to die on the cross for me. Lord, I just ask one more time, forgive my sins and help me see light in the middle of this dark feeling I hold inside. Show me the way, Lord. Search in my mind and my heart, Lord, and help understand why I fall. What is your purpose in my life at this point, Lord? Just help me understand and open my eyes to the light you are trying to show me, O Lord. In Jesus's name, amen.

Search for the Lord and for his strength; continually seek him.
1 Chronicles 16:11 NLT

Clay

During college, ministry training, faith-based instruction, and spiritual formation were not part of my curriculum. I was, however, required to take humanities courses within the requirements of my degree in liberal arts, and sure enough, my outlook became liberal and nothing like how I had been raised, Christian and Pentecostal. I turned into a person I never knew I could be.

When I went home and would talk to my parents about some of the things I was experiencing at school, my dad would tell me, "I know, and just because I don't say anything about it doesn't mean I approve your behavior." He knew I wasn't the Christian preacher's daughter he raised me to be. I didn't know how to explain how things had spiraled out of control, and he never asked, "Why?" "What happened?" or "What changed?" To protect me, my parents tried to warn me about my friends and tell me who to not befriend, but I was sure not to blame my friends for my conduct.

Our relationship suffered in other ways too. I enjoyed the sun. But if I got too much sun, my mom would tell me, "You look like clay." Perhaps the color of my burned skin or the evidence of sin in my life was changing my outward appearance, and she didn't hesitate to say it. It was funny to my friends, because Mom would translate her Spanish thoughts into English, so it would sound odd to them. But I got what she was saying.

Then, when I began to put on weight in college, the typical freshman fifteen turned to twenty and thirty pounds eventually. Mom would tell me if she thought I was eating too much, and she would attempt to help me find weight-loss supplements. As soon as I would visit family, the first thing they would comment on was my weight. College didn't always feel like a sweet escape, but I felt better when I was away because student engagement and living with my friends provided a greater sense of belonging.

My parents worked arduously to support my college expenses, and my mother would warn me that any mistake—such as pregnancy, as she would say— could cost my future and career opportunities. She encouraged me to remain focused, limit my social life, and turn off my phone's text-messaging capability to cut back on distractions. It was a vain attempt to socially distance me from my friends.

Your own ears will hear him.
Right behind you a voice will say,
"This is the way you should go,"
whether to the right or to the left.
Isaiah 30:21 NLT

My Prayer Journal: August 8, 2005

Dear God,

I have sinned. Please forgive me. I am struggling with sexual desires, alcohol, my language usage, and many other feelings that I know are not coming from you. God, I just need you to know what I feel is hunger for you. I need to feel loved. I need you to fill that hole that I know sex, any man, alcohol, cigarettes, and even friends cannot fill. I need you, Lord. I pray that you keep me shielded from worldly passions and that you teach me as I read this book. Lord, help me, but most importantly, I ask that you forgive me. Teach me to recognize and accept when I need to say NO!

Satan has deceived me. He has told me through many thoughts and friends in many "pretty" ways, "We are not perfect," "It takes mistakes and experiences to grow," "We need to enjoy ourselves because college only comes once in a lifetime," and "God is merciful and understanding, so why not follow the desires of my heart with good emotions?" He has played with my mind and lied to me in a very clever and "pretty" way. Please, Lord, help me learn to discern when the devil is lying to me.

I know you already know that slimy little lizard who is up on my shoulder constantly. Yes, sex, lust, language, music, friends, boy craziness, anger, sadness, impatience, frustrations—you know it all, my Lord. I know you are the only one who can help me, Lord. Without you I am helpless. I need you, Lord, because I am fearful. I know the end is coming soon, and how sad I would be if you came and I stayed. Lord, I feel so alone. I am hurt. I am so sad, Lord.

And yes, the devil has lied to me and I have been running away. I've been feeling so ashamed, pathetic, and miserable. Especially when I look at other youth like Vivianna and Karina (church friends), girls that I know may have their hardships, but I know you keep them and save them from falling. Lord, I need change. I need you to renew me. I need you to move me to a different level. I need you to help me in my decisions and the situations I experienced this past summer. Lord help me say NO! Lord, I need you once again. Amen.

Fools make fun of guilt, but the godly acknowledge it and seek reconciliation.
Proverbs 14:9

Addicted

Ironically, the guy I had broken up with at the end of my first year in college suggested that I read "I Kissed Dating Goodbye" by Joshua Harris. If you ask me today what I took away from this book, all I can say is that I was inspired to pray, seek, and know a way out of my own demise, my own heart's desires. I asked God to forgive me for having a divided heart. I continued to ask the Lord to help me give my heart completely to Him. I begged the Lord to return my hopes and dreams to me.

I still desired to be with someone, but I wanted the Lord to bring that person to me. I asked Him to cast these wrong desires into the depths of the ocean. I knew that anyone who had been a part of my life up to that point was not the person God had for me. I wanted those desires to be replaced with a desire for God to be the center. I didn't want a summer fling.

Talking to God about my heart and the past helped me realize that I had my heart and mind in the wrong places before. I recognized I was jumping into situations without careful thought. My emotions were driving me to make decisions I regretted. I thought it was too late to go back. I had faith that God had a purpose in my life, but I didn't know how to let go of negative thoughts, negative feelings, and negative influence around me.

I was sad and angry with myself, and I asked God to take those things away. I asked Him to make things go His way, but something still wasn't adding up. I was still telling God what to do by asking Him for things that were not according to His will—a relationship. Why was that so heavy on my heart, and why couldn't I let that go? I thought I could mend my ways by doing something different.

I would pay it forward, I decided. Before returning to MBC, a friend from church invited us over for dinner so I could speak to her daughter about college. I took Joshua Harris's book with me. I thought, *"She is two years younger than me. I can help her."* We waited about three hours for her to come home from work, and as soon as the door opened, I heard a voice I recognized. Along with her, in walked the fellow from church that I had spent my summer days talking to, secretly hanging out with late into the night behind my parent's back. I was crushed. All I could do was the coward thing: breathe in, breathe out, relax, and watch how her mom acted toward him.

On our drive home, I talked to Mom and Dad about it briefly. I cried and confessed to them that it was as if something was taken from me. I really liked him, and after all, he was going to our church. My parents didn't know, but they empathized with me. It upset Dad a bit, and I remember feeling the urgency to tell our pastor. Dad did not have such a good vibe about this guy and had warned me not to entertain his charm, but I did not listen. Dad suspected the guy wanted to charm all the girls in church, particularly two of us.

That Sunday, I approached the pastor and asked to share something with him. He seemed a bit perplexed after I told him the guy had been sweet-talking me and another girl from the church and that the other girl's mom was ok with her daughter having a relationship with him after all. Nonetheless limited on awareness of the situation. Even so, my friend and the fellow continued dating. Sadly, she was allowed to marry this guy shortly after she graduated high school. Later, when I found out via Facebook photos that my pastor was the one who married them, I was completely done trusting ministers.

I did a self-evaluation and reflected on my prayer life. I realized I was going to crash and burn if I did not turn away from sin. I always wanted to make God a part of my mess rather than being a part of His order for my life. I had my priorities mixed up. I prayed and asked God to make me pure again, to make me whole, and to help me accept the things He had for me. This was a vicious cycle I didn't understand, and I couldn't figure a way out of it. I recognize today that my prayers were fueled by selfish, vain thoughts. I wanted God to bless me, but I didn't want to let go of the one thing I was addicted to—feeling loved.

I had already failed with my lips. I had spoken of desires that were wrong, and I had once again trusted the wrong person with those feelings. I had become remorseful but not repentant. If I would have been repentant, I would have made the changes I needed to make. Instead, I was sabotaging my own destiny by professing one thing and doing another.

How could this happen? How could this be? For when I planted you, I chose my seed so carefully—the very best. Why have you become this degenerate race of evil men? No amount of soap or lye can make you clean. You are stained with guilt that cannot ever be washed away. I see it always before me, the Lord God says. You say it isn't so, that you haven't worshiped idols? How can you say a thing like that? Go and look in any valley in the land! Face the awful sins that you have done, O restless female camel, seeking for a male! You are a wild donkey, sniffing the wind at mating time. (Who can restrain your lust?) Any jack wanting you need not search, for you come running to him! Why don't you turn from all this weary running after other gods? But you say, "Don't waste your breath. I've fallen in love with these strangers and I can't stop loving them now!"

Jeremiah 2:21–25 TLB

My Prayer Journal: September 27, 2005

Dear Lord,

It's been such a long time since I've prayed and asked you for anything. I am sad, Lord. I am so upset. Where has my faith and fear of God gone? I am a drinker and a smoker. I am a fornicator and a liar. Lord, what have I been doing to myself, to you? I don't even know where to begin. Oh Lord, please forgive me. I have left you and abandoned my own spirit. I have forgotten how to run to you in moments of temptation.

I need help, Lord. I really do. I need you in my life and don't even know where to begin asking. Oh Lord, I need you. I am empty yet so full of happiness in this world. I forget daily that you are the One and only that I need. Lord, show me where I should be. Tell me, oh Lord, what I should be and where I should go. Point me in the right direction, but Lord, let it be you and not someone who just wants to judge me. Amen.

Seek the Lord, all who are humble, and follow his commands. Seek to do what is right and to live humbly. Perhaps even yet the Lord will protect you—protect you from his anger on that day of destruction.

Zephaniah 2:3 NLT

World Traveler

I really didn't like physically running, but if I could get on a plane, I was ready to fly! At the end of my sophomore year, I traveled to Germany, Holland, France, and Prague for three weeks with my world geography cohort under the instruction and guidance of one MBC professor.

This trip brought back memories of my time growing up overseas and reminded me of those times my family took trips throughout Europe. I attempted to connect with the people I knew in Holland during my three days in Amsterdam, but they had moved to Rotterdam. I was aware that some of the students on the trip were finding enjoyment, within their legal right, of enjoying sinful pleasure. Meanwhile, deep within me, I knew we were in the center of a dark place that my family would visit with the purpose of evangelizing when I was a child. I did not express these thoughts solely because I agreeably participated in the nightlife ambiance and drinking. I justified myself by saying that I would be a hypocrite if I dared to preach about wrongdoing with a drink or a cigarette in my hand.

The remorse always made me want to go back to that time and make different choices—say something, do something—but I was too deep in sin. I knew that autonomy did not equal a license to sin and that I would face consequences for my own choices regardless of what my parents approved or disapproved of. The little understanding I had about grace was diminishing, and I was on the road to self-pity. I was at a point of no return.

Jesus answered them, "Truly, truly, I say to you, everyone who practices sin is a slave to sin." John 8:34 ESV

Ciao, Bella

By the end of my junior year at MBC, I had moved off campus. I was working at the college admissions office as a tele-counselor and living in my own apartment with my roommate, Erica. One thing that made Erica special was our mutual understanding that one day we would get it together and that God was at the center of our hearts despite our shortcomings. Something about her made me feel closer to home and God, and she never judged me for knowing what I knew but still making the choices I would make. She was easy-going and a great listener, and we enjoyed cooking, shopping, working, and just talking.

Then, while spending my first summer away from home, I decided to take a statistics class at the local community college. While registering for the course, I stumbled across a catalogue from The American Institute for Foreign Studies. At that moment, nothing was in question for me, I felt confident about traveling overseas, and I quickly sensed an open door to ask my parents if I could count on their support to go.

I called my mom at the Pentagon, knowing she would move mountains to make that dream a possibility. My brother was stationed in Pensacola, Florida (he had enlisted in the United States Marine Corps six months prior), and I knew that staying in Virginia just wasn't cutting it for me. I was getting bored of college life and continuous chaos due to my own choices.

As soon as I knew that I would be spending my senior year in college away in Europe, I sublet my half of the lease, packed, went back to my usual summer job at the Pentagon, and obtained my passport, visa, and financial support as I prepared to move. The only thing I recall left pending for when I would return was my goal to graduate and commission into the United States Marine Corps for Officer Candidate School. Some dreams were beginning to return to me.

While studying abroad through Richmond University of London in Rome, Italy, I felt urgency to rediscover the correct path I should take. My dad had warned me about possible dangers and measures I should take to stay safe. Suddenly, risk taking was not an option when it came to going out with friends, and I made it my priority to play by the rules overseas. I no longer wanted to be so liberal about the very things that could cost a big price.

With my college graduation and career choices around the corner, I considered my options. In fact, it was during my fall semester abroad that I heard about the murder in Perugia, Italy. I had experienced some of the frustrations that come with heavy drinking back home and I did not want to wind up locked up abroad, let alone dead. I took every precaution from the program office and *Carabinieri* (Italian police) to enjoy the time and make lasting memories, but it did not stop me from finding the popular *Café Caruso*, where I would frequent for salsa nights. In addition to my involvement in most Italian cultural immersion activities from cooking class, excursions through the Amalfi Coast, Venice, and Tuscany, wine-tasting and happy hour with Italians, my passion for Latin music and salsa dancing was known throughout the school.

Still, I hadn't given ministry any more thought since my high school days. How could I with all the iniquity that clouded my vision and consumed my soul? I didn't consider that I could trace the same places apostles, like Paul and Peter, walked during their ministry and my fundamental values would be too blurred to grasp these meaningful moments.

I was taking classes in art history and religion in Rome. My mom came to visit me in Italy. While visiting the prison where the apostle Paul was kept, Mamertine, I became inspired to study more biblical history, but it was not because of an understanding of my purpose. Rather, it was something in me reaching for what I wouldn't understand until much later down the road (how much I would admire the apostles, their ministry, and the roads they traversed would be imperative for me to learn in order to get through some of my fiery trials).

I ventured throughout the inner city and the suburbs of Rome to visit the cathedrals dedicated to the saints. It was not part of my curriculum plan while I was studying, but it felt so right to dig deeper into my inquisitive nature, and it was fun with Mom, my childhood Sunday school teacher. It was then that I could feel a sense of relationship with her that only when we were off to an adventure we could truly embrace.

This was the first time I learned about martyrdom and suffering for the sake of Christ. History was one of my favorite subjects throughout all of school, and only while I was living in Europe did I learn to treasure the value of history. It was while living in Europe that my curiosity for more knowledge of Christianity and history were actually birthed. I began searching for a Hispanic ministry in Rome and located one in the outskirts of the city center. On a few occasions I went and even took Mom with me during her visit. I wanted to seek, I wanted to reconnect with church, and I was searching for my niche.

I lived two blocks from the Colosseum in Rome. Walking or taking a bus or train were my favorite things to do for a cappuccino at *Il Bar*, a pizza at Rosso *Pomodoro*, my favorite Greek salad at *L'insala Ricca*, or a pit stop at the local grocery store, *Despar*. This was one of the times in my life I had experienced fewer vulnerabilities and immense joy because I was far away from home in a different chapter in history. I could not have asked for a better senior year in college.

My brother requested leave from duty and came to visit me with Mom and Dad during spring semester. Dad brought up the time when I had the upset look on my face on the family photo we took at the Colosseum because it was moments after he embarrassed me with his public display of correction. I did not give it my full attention. I preferred to enjoy my time with them walking through museums, the Roman Forum, and attempting to bond for the first time in a long time. Toward the end of their visit, things became tense once again because by that time, my family had grown apart in affection and appreciation for different things. Mom and Dad headed to their hotel to call it a night, and my brother and I spent more time hanging out with my study-abroad friends at on the streets of *Campo di Fiori* in Rome.

On the night of my twenty-second birthday celebration, we headed to *Caruso* and I recall crying on my friend Rocio's shoulder, saying, "I have no idea what I'll do with my life after we graduate." It was as if a part of me was being taken, my freedom and spirit of adventure. My brother and all my friends hugged me.

I was two months away from returning to the States to graduate MBC yet frightened at the thought that I would not be able to go into the military as I hoped. I was having a difficult time with running and weight loss even though I had a gym membership overseas and trained frequently. I never liked running. I thought, *I am going to become stagnant, deal with hectic traffic in D.C., work as a civilian, and get stuck paying bills and living without fulfillment*. I would have to be willing to surrender everything I knew if I wanted to continue living the life I preferred in Europe, and that was not an option. I considered skipping my flight, but I knew my visa would expire. It was just a matter of time.

Upon my return to the States, I graduated and accepted the first job I landed, working with my dad in Arlington, Virginia. Two weeks after accepting that civilian job that I did not have a desire for, I resigned to accept a job as an admissions counselor at MBC. Afterall, it was easier to return to Staunton and my plan B if all else failed. I did not want to live with my parents after living away for four years. My Big Sista Rissa (from MBC) thought I was crazy for turning down a government civilian job, living at home with my parents, and a free ride to work for less money and more entertainment. My thought process did not make sense to others.

Suddenly, it dawned on me that my mom had told me, "As soon as you graduate, I am going to try to go to Germany again." She was right. By August 2008, my parents were on their way back to Germany three months after my college graduation. Mom had accepted a new job overseas. This was not so unfortunate for me as you may be thinking, because for my parents it would be a new chapter overseas and for me an excuse to travel and visit anytime. After all, my next goal at twenty-two was to go to Officer Candidate School with the United States Marine Corps and travel.

CHAPTER FOUR

The Gypsy

*Don't worry about the wicked or envy those who do wrong.
For like grass, they soon fade away. Like spring
flowers, they soon wither. Trust in the Lord and do
good. Then you will live safely in the land and
prosper. Take delight in the Lord, and he will give
you your heart's desires. Commit everything
you do to the Lord. Trust him, and he will help you.
Psalm 37:1–5 NLT*

Road Runner

My Big Sista Rissa gifted me with a jewelry box with my name engraved in bold letters and said, "I chose that because I always considered you to be bold, Botyla!" Shortly after graduating, we met for dinner and drinks at a restaurant in Northern Virginia. I shared with her my intent to leave the job I had recently started with a government contract, for an offer to work in the admissions office at MBC. We planned to spend as much time together on the weekends when I traveled up to D.C. with Isabella, my pug.

To my surprise, two of my best friends from Germany, came to my graduation and left inspired to pursue their college education. At that moment I discovered not everything was a distant memory of the past; I had found purpose in motivating and encouraging others to realize their dreams. Little did I know that my former boss of just two weeks, Mr. Bell, whom I had met with before leaving to work for MBC, was also contacting the admissions office. Mr. Bell's daughter was also one of my perspective students for enrollment the following year. The world was becoming smaller, and my purpose was growing again.

I loved my college, and I was loyal to our vision and mission as a community striving for academic excellence. But women empowerment was also on the rise, and I did not see myself as someone fighting for women's rights or feminism, but I was on a broad path of accepting every challenge to excel, empower other women, and prove I was strong and independent from what any man could tell me. The belief that success was attainable was ever increasing as I witnessed more young women take on the challenge of higher education and complete their degrees. I considered myself to be resourceful and proud to celebrate their achievements. You see, I believed, if I could do it, so could they, because I never believed it for myself until I walked across the stage as a first-generation college graduate as a minority woman. Today I understand why I could have been "Boldly Baldwin" while remaining humble unto God, but I still resembled that spirit of Jezebel whom my brother once called me with my ego.

"But as for the cowardly, the faithless, the detestable, as for murderers, the sexually immoral, sorcerers, idolaters, and all liars, their portion will be in the lake that burns with fire and sulfur, which is the second death."
Revelation 21:8, ESV

The time I spent working in admissions at MBC was productive to say the least. I was devoted to exercising, building relationships with my sisters who remained at the college for their senior year, and determined to pursue the Marine Corps. I traveled to various college fairs for recruitment throughout Virginia and

North Carolina. I enjoyed being a road runner. Afterall, staying in one place for too long was my least favorite thing to do.

I was always ranting and raving about my personal trainer, my goals, weight-loss achievements, and how independent I felt after my parents left for Germany. Not to mention, Titi Carmen and I reconnected after seven years of separation. Normarie and Tito were living in Northern Virginia. Normarie had graduated high school, and my desire was to see her succeed at anything she put her mind to—school, work, and love. I made myself available to her as much as I could so that we could rekindle lost time and never lose touch again.

Though the intent and effort were never in vain, I was unsuccessful at convincing my family to reconcile their differences. Once again, I was told by Dad, "Don't worry about that, and don't try to convince anyone of anything." It was as if my family did not have hope for repairing and restoring relationships, but my outlook was different. I kept those thoughts to myself and continued my own path until the next opportunity for reconciliation.

Still, my friends could not understand why I had become liberal about my ways in the social and relationship spectrum and how I could be so careless when it came to moral decisions. They attempted to talk sense to me, telling me, "Boty, this is not you." I became divided in my thoughts, not realizing that I had forsaken my fundamental Christian values and that if I did not change, it would cost me something greater. Who was I? Who did I serve? I missed Italy, I missed being able to visit my parents on a moment's notice, and I was attempting to play the role of "Ms. Independent."

Don't you realize that those who do wrong will not inherit the Kingdom of God? Don't fool yourselves. Those who indulge in sexual sin, or who worship idols, or commit adultery, or are male prostitutes, or practice homosexuality, or are thieves, or greedy people, or drunkards, or are abusive, or cheat people—none of these will inherit the Kingdom of God. Some of you were once like that.

But you were cleansed; you were made holy; you were made right with God by calling
on the name of the Lord Jesus Christ and by the Spirit of our God.
1 Corinthians 6:9–11 NLT

Detoured

A mutual friend from college re-introduced me to a high school classmate, Charles, whom she now worked with at a bank. I was now faced with opposition from my dad regarding the military (he wanted me to get married and start a family instead), but I still gave training my best shot and submitted my application for Officer Candidate School. I studied for the Armed Services Vocational Aptitude Battery and dedicated myself to work, gym, and studying. I settled for not renewing my contract with MBC and decided to go to Europe to stay with my parents the upcoming summer.

As I prepared for the Medical Evaluation Processing Station (MEPS) appointment in June 2009, I was already giving up on the idea of joining the Marine Corps. I knew my dad didn't want me to and neither did Charles. At MEPS, I gave up on the dream based on not meeting the weight standard by three pounds and wanting to please my family by doing what I vowed to never do: move back to Northern Virginia and get married right after college.

While I was with my parents for the summer in Germany, my dad kept asking me if Charles and I were going to get married. Charles came to visit and meet my parents, and within six months of starting dating, we retraced my old stomping grounds in Rome, Italy, and I showed him the extravagant life in Europe. Under the scorching heat of the sun, and pressure of time, he proposed marriage to me without my dad's blessing. The next months with him were fueled with fights and drama ranging from the smallest bouts of jealousy to insecurities with pornography, ex-girlfriends, and lies.

Though we were engaged and planning a sixty-thousand-dollar wedding, my fears drove me to the church I visited during my breaks at home from college. On one of those occasions, the pastor's daughter approached me as I got off my knees at the altar and said to me, "I have to tell you something. If I don't, I'm afraid

I would be disobeying the Lord. God does not want you to be unequally yoked."
With tears flowing down my face, I hesitated to maintain the relationship, but the
financial investment and the remorse for having to start over was keeping me bound.

My friend Nienke said, "Congratulations, Boty. You got your shut-up ring!"
Other friends were shocked because they recalled me telling them what I did not
want, but I was convinced that this was the right thing to do. After all, "shacking up
is not the correct thing to do," according to my dad. My parents were in Germany,
my brother was headed to a deployment, and I was living independently. Sure, I
wanted to please my parents and I was adamant about doing what I believed was
best, but what about my Father in heaven?

Honor your father and your mother, that your days may be long upon the land which
the Lord your God is giving you.
Exodus 20:12

Childish, Insecure, Yeller

I shared my past with my fiancé, telling him everything. I struggled with
how this affected our relationship because when we would argue, we would throw
the past in each other's face. I didn't know how to have a relationship. I had never
been allowed to, and when I did, the guy was so nice that it scared me. I thought,
"This is too good to be true."

But why was I so afraid of trusting? I had known the best and the worst;
the best were the ones that were scared off and the worse professed to be Christian
men of God. I began going to professional counseling. It was that or no relationship
because I needed to discover my own perspective on marriage. I did not know how
to seek this from a biblical perspective.

Church was not a part of our life and every time I suggested we should
go, my fiancé would say, "You can go." I had already shared my deepest fears with
him—infidelity, and divorce—but church was a distant thought for him. I always
said that I did not want to get married. I feared marriage would end in a divorce
because I had known even ministers who committed adultery but never got caught.

Nothing guaranteed me that it would not happen to me, and I had big trust issues. My biggest reason for my way of thinking was fear, and I never hesitated to say it. I was never too sure that I would not become another statistic. But with my desire to please my parents and do what I thought was right, I attempted to please everyone while slowly becoming a victim of my own demise.

Insecure, childish, and yeller became my new names. That is what Charles called me when I suspected he was either cheating on me or not telling me the truth about something. We didn't go to church together many times in the three years we were together, but we did complete premarital counseling classes at my dad's suggestion. We began to follow the normative of a Christian couple, but we both knew we were only holding onto the little positivity that stemmed from our mutual friends' support.

After several sessions with my counselor, I decided to tell my parents what took place during my high school years—who, what, where, how, and when. To my surprise, my parents didn't rebuke me, disown me, or judge me. They felt hurt, betrayed, and sad, and Mom said, "It was not your fault." My dad said, "I don't want to know the details, I just don't ever want to see him." I was relieved but not certain this would never come back up again.

On August 9, 2010, my fiancé and I got married at the Salvation Army in Ponce, Puerto Rico, just like my parents had done on July 3, 1982. But Charles said, "We will never be like your parents."

I followed my heart one decision after another. I managed to complete a master's degree in Human Resource Management while working at DeVry University, attempted and failed at marriage, lost my job, and filed for bankruptcy, forsaking yet another dream: a historical Victorian home in the heart of the Shenandoah Valley where I could freely return to visit MBC as an alumna.

No matter how much my husband and I had accomplished together, the uphill battles and the countless losses were the result of uncalculated risk and choices God had never been a part of. I had a faithless life full of anger, resentment, and sorrow because what I had envisioned seemed impossible. I had been unable to get pregnant, which I thought could solve our issues. I attempted going to church, going to counseling, and confiding in my work friends, but nothing changed my reality. I had disobeyed the Lord and His warning. I had ignored the red flags. Now I was getting divorced.

Jesus knew their thoughts and said to them: "Any kingdom divided against itself will be ruined, and a house divided against itself will fall."
Luke 11:17 NIV

With the most lasting impression coming from my ex-husband's words, "You just want to write a story," I remembered that moment on the streets of Rome when I realized I would have to lose everything in order to gain. On those same streets, I had given up one more opportunity to render my entire life to Him by giving it away to a fantasy in August 2009.

My story was only beginning to develop. The Word always reminded me, "And what do you benefit if you gain the whole world but lose your own soul? Is anything worth more than your soul?" (Matthew 16:26 NLT). I knew my soul was in need of immediate repair. Despite the detour I had taken, I was convinced that if I began seeking a voice from heaven for direction and gave away everything, then moved to South Florida, I would experience and encounter with my creator.

Divorced, Bankrupt, and Unemployed

In September 2013, when I was twenty-seven, all my dreams came crashing down. Every door I encountered was slammed in my face. The military, the job I would learn I couldn't return to, and even my Plan C of going into the police force were rejected. My biggest fear became my reality. I was divorced, bankrupt, unemployed, and traumatized.

As tears streamed down my face, I received a phone call regarding a job at Nova Southeastern University (NSU) in Miami. I had applied for this job one year prior and thought the opportunity had passed. In a matter of days, I was on a flight to Fort Lauderdale. I thought, *I might be alone on this new journey, but it will be worth the change.*

I wasn't concerned about keeping any of my possessions. I wanted to start all over again. My parents and my uncle drove from Alabama to Virginia to help me move. We loaded up my Mini Cooper and my uncle's truck and headed down I-95 to my brother's house in North Carolina for a night of rest. Two years prior I had desired to move to Florida, and it was now becoming a reality.

I wasn't afraid of moving alone, but I also wasn't aware of the new challenges ahead. Dad told me to stay close to him on the highway because we used a utility trailer to transport my things. About an hour after my mom and I arrived at my brother's house, my uncle and my dad arrived. My dad yelled at me, "If you don't listen to me, you will end up by yourself," along with some choice words I won't add. Though he apologized that night, I realized I was already alone, and he had no idea this "gypsy" had one earnest desire: to meet God again.

'So I say to you: Ask and it will be given to you; seek and you will find; knock and the door will be opened to you. For everyone who asks receives; the one who seeks finds; and to the one who knocks, the door will be opened. Which of you fathers, if your son asks for a fish, will give him a snake instead?"

Luke 11:9–11 NIV

CHAPTER FIVE

The Prodigal Daughter

"And he arose and came to his father. But when he was still a great way off, his father saw him and had compassion, and ran and fell on his neck and kissed him. And the son said to him, 'Father, I have sinned against heaven and in your sight, and am no longer worthy to be called your son.' But the father said to his servants, 'Bring out the best robe and put it on him and put a ring on his hand and sandals on his feet. And bring the fatted calf here and kill it and let us eat and be merry; for this my son was dead and is alive again; he was lost and is found.' And they began to be merry."

Luke 15:20–24

Sweet Home Alabama

I attempted pursuing other job opportunities in Alabama, although I hoped for the offer from NSU in Florida. Grateful, and challenged to press on, I visited Pinkard Baptist Church with my uncle and his wife during my time with them in Dothan, the Peanut Capital of Alabama.

I instantly felt a pulling from God to seek Him in the midst of my transition. This was the first time since 2004 that my family was afforded the opportunity to be together in a congregation. I remember Dad always said, "The Bible says to not forsake the assemblies." I admit, I was upset that he was no longer as enthusiastic about much. He was undergoing some transitional challenges topped by a recent diagnosis of cancer and moving back to the States—first to Massachusetts and then to Alabama shortly thereafter. Mom, on the other hand, had retired and was attempting to finish school while supporting the family during challenging times of transition. I was convinced that I wanted to seek a relationship with God and total restoration.

Willing to accept a step-down from my previous position as campus financial aid manager, I accepted a job as a counselor at NSU and began searching for a place to live in Davie, Florida. The time I spent seeking and planning my move was filled with anxiety. Some of my family said that worse things awaited me in South Florida, such as sin, witchcraft, and temptation. I felt the naysayers would never stop speaking and I needed to remain focused. I wanted to move forward and knew there was nothing left for me to consider about where I should live or go for work.

While watching a livestream service on Enlace TV with my mom, I realized that one of my favorite singers from my high school days, Christian singer Julissa, was leading worship at a church in Miami. Her perseverance in the Lord inspired me, and I came to see that I was missing out on something I once felt passionate about: publicly giving praise and adoration to God. I exclaimed, "I am going to Miami, and I'm going to find me a mega church, get plugged in, and focus on God and my restoration!"

Through the Lord's mercies we are not consumed, because His compassions fail not.
They are new every morning; great is Your faithfulness.
Lamentations 3:22–23

On Saturday, January 4, 2014, I arrived in South Florida for a fresh start. My newfound cousins welcomed me into their home for a few weeks as I transitioned to my new apartment and job at NSU. The next day, I rededicated my life to God by making a commitment that I would honor what I said when I left Alabama. My realtor friend Brandon helped me with the apartment process and with getting acquainted with the best food spots and beachfronts.

Two weeks later, upon receiving the keys to my apartment, I prayed and thanked God for His mercies and provision. My transition to Florida was fully covered financially and I had a plan in place to pay back the money I borrowed from my dad for that to become a reality. I was at peace with my decisions. Proverbs 15:16 was the word that came to my heart at this time: "Better is a little with the fear of the Lord, than great treasure with trouble."

My Prayer Journal: January 13, 2014

Dear God,

I am so thankful for the blessings and the abundance you have graced me with. I want to thank you for bringing me out of Virginia and safely taking me to my family in Alabama. I want to thank you for the opportunities with NSU. I also want to thank you because during this transition, you have not left me alone. Thank you for family, friends, and for everyone you have placed in my life with purpose.

Lord, I write to you and pray because I am constantly searching for your direction, your peace, and your guidance. Even if you don't give me answers or explain anything to me, I trust you and your purpose for my life. I am blessed every day that I wake up and have food to eat and a way to get around. I am so thankful, God, but I am not perfect. I come to you now and ask you to forgive me of my doubts and fears. I'm not sure I can go to anyone else anymore.

I need you. I always need you, but right now, I'm uncertain if you've placed anyone else in my life for a good cause. I'm not sure how to say any of this. I just need your direction. God, I am so scared. I want your protection over me. I need your protection at home, on the street, at work, and anywhere I go. I have been told many things, good and bad. I just want to know that no matter what, you are by my side and you are guiding me and protecting me with every step I take.

Those who live in the shelter of the Most High will find rest in the shadow of the Almighty. This I declare about the Lord: He alone is my refuge, my

place of safety; he is my God, and I trust him. or he will rescue
you from every trap and protect you from deadly disease.
He will cover you with his feathers. He will shelter you
with his wings. His faithful promises are your armor and
protection. Do not be afraid of the terrors of the night,
nor the arrow that flies in the day.
Psalm 91:1–5 NLT

Vain

I appreciate the way John Ortberg described Saturdays in his book, *Who Is This Man?* "Everybody knows Saturday. Saturday is the day your dream died. You wake up and you're still alive, you must go on, but you don't know how. Worse, you don't know why. The hope and joy are nonexistent." When I woke up one Saturday, I realized Florida is like a wilderness with sunny skies and pretty blue water.

During my first six months there I met a lot of people, frequently visited new places, and enjoyed the peace that came with my transition. I believed I had the best job, the best place to live, and the best surrounding areas to reflect, soak up the sun, and dream again. Then I became lonely. No one could offer me encouragement. Some recommended I do disappointment management and gave me simplistic explanations. Others told me I didn't have enough faith. The hardest advice was from the one who told me to "wait."

I was always waiting. During the great escape from the pain of my past mistakes, I searched for restoration and rebuilding, and I arrived in a wilderness of temptation. I was lost, and discovered I was no different than other people selfishly seeking and chasing vain ideologies. The worst part was always feeling alone. Once again, my mind was full of chaos and confusion. In my heart and mind, I was convinced that a new place would define a new me. Most of the time I felt lonely, guilty, and sorry for myself. I gradually dug myself into a pit of depression with my thought patterns.

If you think you are standing strong, be careful not to fall. The temptations in your life are no different from what others experience. And God is faithful. He will not allow the temptation to be more than you can stand. When you are tempted, he will show you a way out so that you can endure.

1 Corinthians 10:12–14 NLT

I found myself thinking, "There is a way, and I have to turn around and go back that way before it's too late." I desired something like what I had been accustomed to during my childhood and teenage years—church, Bible groups, and ministry. But I didn't fit in anymore. For some I was too spiritual, for others I was too tainted.

You say, "I am allowed to do anything"—but not everything is good for you. And even though "I am allowed to do anything," I must not become a slave to anything. You say, "Food was made for the stomach, and the stomach for food." (This is true, though someday God will do away with both of them.) But you can't say that our bodies were made for sexual immorality. They were made for the Lord, and the Lord cares about our bodies. And God will raise us from the dead by his power, just as he raised our Lord from the dead. Run from sexual sin! No other sin so clearly affects the body as this one does. For sexual immorality is a sin against your own body. Don't you realize that your body is the temple of the Holy Spirit, who lives in you and was given to you by God? You do not belong to yourself, for God bought you with a high price. So, you must honor God with your body.

2 Corinthians 6:12–20 NLT

The sadness intensified and every time I felt more disconnected from God's children, I sought more connection with the community outside the church building. The Enemy always had an alternative waiting for me to accept when I was at my lowest. Ironically, the very people I would draw near to would push me away because I never fit in.

I had countless arguments about the Bible and my beliefs. I defended my testimony at all hours of the night with friends or cousins. The confrontation of who I had become and who I really wanted to be was evident, and my friends couldn't stand my approach. Conversations I started in good faith ended in an argument. I felt as though I was shadowboxing with faith and Scripture. I didn't even believe everything I was saying anymore. I felt defenseless, but something told me God understood me, so I hoped for His rescue. But how could I preach what I was not convinced of? I wanted to defend my own cause, but Jesus was waiting on me to accept Him without reservations.

Regardless of the places I had moved to and from; the schools I'd attended; the church I was affiliated with; my friends, coworkers, and community; or the statutes I stood for, I still lacked understanding of who I was and who I represented. People could see right through me, or my Facebook for that matter. I was attempting to live a purpose-driven life with a fancy label. I wanted to live as a Christian, but I felt inadequate and unacceptable through their lenses. My attitude did not match my words. My actions did not match my intentions. I misjudged everything, and I questioned my salvation and if God was still my Father.

Truly, truly, I say to you, whoever believes has eternal life.
John 6:47 ESV

Misunderstood

In an attempt to reach closure with my past, in 2015 I sought yet another professional counselor. I shared the darkest and deepest frustrations I'd experienced in my past and began to talk about the unresolved issues of division and dysfunction with my family. I felt I was unable to properly channel my feelings, and I would always resort to wine and whining as I traveled down memory lane going through the list of memories and discovering that my parents' unrealistic expectations were tormenting me. No matter how hard I tried, I felt that I hadn't accomplished much or even warranted their praise. I was suffocated by unresolved matters and wanted to run once again.

Who has anguish? Who has sorrow?
Who is always fighting? Who is always complaining?
Who has unnecessary bruises? Who has bloodshot eyes?
It is the one who spends long hours in the taverns,
trying out new drinks.
Don't gaze at the wine, seeing how red it is,
how it sparkles in the cup, how smoothly it goes down.

For in the end it bites like a poisonous snake;
it stings like a viper.
You will see hallucinations,
and you will say crazy things.
You will stagger like a sailor tossed at sea,
clinging to a swaying mast.
And you will say, "They hit me, but I didn't feel it.
I didn't even know it when they beat me up.
When will I wake up
so I can look for another drink?"
Proverbs 23:29–35 NLT

I argued with myself and my family about my choices—from marrying too fast, to filing for bankruptcy as a result, to what I did in my spare time from work, who I dated, what church I went to, and what doctrines I was following, to which family members I should stay away from. Nothing I did was enough to bring about the peace I was seeking. I was conflicted by my convictions. I was told so many things I didn't want to hear, things about my character, my attitude, and my outlook on life, marriage, and family. My dad told me, "It's as if you take one step forward and ten backwards." His perception of me was incorrect. I was reaching for something different, something that I had yet to experience—love and kindness.

I was confused. I praised the ground my parents walked on. Yet we couldn't last a day without an argument or a disagreement followed by deep apathy and pain.

I would hear the two dreadful phrases from my dad, "You should . . ." or "You need to . . ." and my mom would quote from a tombstone in Spanish: "How you look is how I looked, and how you see me is how you will look." What? I thought. I couldn't measure up and felt like a disappointment to them. I was continuously believing in thoughts of inadequacy, failure, and turmoil. I wondered, *"Why are other families normal but mine is not? "*

"Fear not, for I am with you; be not dismayed, for I am your God. I will strengthen you, Yes, I will help you, I will uphold you with My righteous right hand."
Isaiah 41:10

Angry

I always thought that, like my grandmother and her younger brother, my older brother and I would end up residing in the same state and build memories to last a lifetime. Not because we were best of friends but because we were close growing up and college, the military, and other unfortunate circumstances kept us apart for ten years. My parents were also living overseas during that time, and we made every attempt to change that when my brother decided to move to Florida.

My parents came to visit us, staying with me in my apartment. I was attempting to show them how far along things had come and how happy I appeared to be. Perhaps my only earnest desire was vain, as the truth would reveal that I just wanted them to be proud of me and know that I could manage things as an adult. After all, my transition to Florida had cost a big price and I was willing to pay my dad back every penny that I could so that he would never have to hold it over my head. I was attempting to make up for my past decisions and prove that I could still be that daughter he raised me to be.

At the same time, I continued accepting invitations to concerts, dinners, or dances from people I was meeting at work and outings. While my brother was preparing to get married and move away to another city with his new family, I was convinced that I was going to remain single and never meet a person adequate for me.

But the night before my parents left, my dad unexpectedly told me, "Let me tell you something. If you get in trouble, don't call me." I was shocked. That same night, he apologized to me, then quoted from Ephesians 4:6, saying, "The Bible says, 'and you, fathers, do not provoke your children to wrath, but bring them up in the training and admonition of the Lord.'"

Even though he apologized, I did not feel that his words came from a loving heart. I did not feel loved unconditionally. At that point, I didn't understand his reasoning or justification for talking to me in that tone in a place I considered my own home. I was angry most of the time with how things were turning with my parents. My dad always told me, "If you need anything and I got it, I will help you." So where was his previous statement to me coming from? I was not in need of monetary support. I needed something different. I desired love, affection, and trust from my parents.

Communication was more like a lecture rather than a conversation. Arguments were always fueled with emotion and interruption until either my dad or I just gave up, walked away, or kept quiet for months at a time. I was convinced that he didn't know how to be who I needed him to be: my dad.

> *My heart has heard you say, "Come and talk with me."*
> *And my heart responds, "Lord, I am coming."*
> *Do not turn your back on me.*
> *Do not reject your servant in anger.*
> *You have always been my helper.*
> *Don't leave me now; don't abandon me,*
> *O God of my salvation!*
> *Even if my father and mother abandon me,*
> *the Lord will hold me close.*
> *Psalm 27:8–10 NLT*

The image I had in my mind was distorted by pain and resentment. I always thought I had received the best upbringing and the best examples from my parents and that I could live up to their standards, but I couldn't be like them—perfect and righteous. Eventually, when my parents returned to Alabama, my mom sent me a message through Facebook, saying that she didn't understand what my problem was with my father and my brother, and that I needed to figure it out because my anger toward men was incomprehensible. I attempted to call my parents on the phone and share with them what my thoughts and concerns were regarding my brother, his sudden decision to get married, and how that affected me.

I had given him my apartment in Davie and moved to another apartment with a roommate because I wanted and believed he would have more comfort where I had originally moved to upon arriving to Florida. Little did I know he would meet someone, get married, and presume I was okay with that. We had both gone through painful divorces the year prior, and I was a bit overprotective to say the least. Though I really liked his new wife and her children, I was convinced that they should not rush. Once again, I was meddling and instigating, and my parents were sure to let me know it was none of my business. That was the moment I knew I was misunderstood and destined for a different path, seeking another way to heal.

After seeking professional counseling over the course of six years and attempting numerous ways to deal with my emotional trauma ranging from the unsettled arguments with my family, to bitterness and resentment toward myself from my own past mistakes and shameful lifestyle, I had yet to discover the implications of some of the details in my past I had to face in order to heal. Some psychologist suggests the following.

According to childtrauma.org, "One out of three females in the U.S., and one out of five males, have been victims of sexual abuse before age 18. And according to the American Academy of Experts in Traumatic Stress (AAETS), 30% of all male children are molested in some way, compared to 40% of females. Some of the most startling statistics unearthed during research into sexual abuse are that children are three times as likely to be victims of rape than adults, and that stranger abuse constitutes by far the minority of cases. It is more likely for a child to experience sexual abuse at the hands of a family member or another supposedly trustworthy adult. Sexual abuse is a truly democratic issue. It affects children and adults across ethnic, socioeconomic, educational, religious, and regional lines."

My constant was talking about it with someone I could trust. I never felt ashamed to share my feelings and my story with people I could sense would listen to me. My biggest problem was always trusting the wrong people. I had been gullible, big mouth, naïve, defensive, abrupt when confronted, and immature. But I always felt better after talking to someone. One thing I could not handle very well was my communication with my family and friends when confronted with the reality of what had happened with me. After all, I had a decent upbringing, generous parents, a loving community in the church, and numerous opportunities afforded to me, education, career, and travel. But I had lost a marriage, the possibility of having a family, children, and a future of hope without true healing. I questioned why in all my Christianity and education; I could not seem to find an answer to my healing.

Let no corrupting talk come out of your mouths, but only such as is good for building
up, as fits the occasion, that it may give grace to those who hear.
Ephesians 4:29 ESV

Work was always a happy place. My boss Brian often called me "young lady." He would talk sense to me, telling me that I was going to ruin my blessing if I kept up with my doubts and what-ifs and didn't remain focused on what is most important, God and faith. He would share his stories about professional experiences, family, and life lessons. I began to learn about the values of mentorship. He helped me be more optimistic and become more grateful about the future ahead without holding onto the past.

I always enjoyed sharing my views and goals with him. He would help me draw up a game plan and brainstorm opportunities while remaining hopeful that things would get better. My coworkers would check on me from time to time. When I struggled, Ms. Julia could see it and she would tell me, "You know what you need to do. Get in the closet and pray to Jesus." They were a light in my life when my family misunderstood me. By the time I worked at DeVry, NVCC, and NSU, I had known four colleagues named Vanessa and each of them were a light in the midst of my darkness. I thank God for their friendship and sincere support.

Get all the advice and instruction you can,
so you will be wise the rest of your life.
You can make many plans,
but the Lord's purpose will prevail.
Proverbs 19:20–21 NLT

Barren

During the spring of 2015, a season of critical thinking and decision making at my workplace, I reached the point that I needed to face the deepest pain of my past and acknowledge how its effect was hindering my growth and perseverance in Christ. As a result of my past experiences in the church, I had attended church only occasionally for over ten years, and I wanted nothing to do with any of the church's expectations, appearances, or rudiments. I didn't trust the church leaders from my earlier attempts to talk about issues perhaps more commonly known of today: emotional abuse, sexual sin, addiction, deliverance, and healing.

Shortly after celebrating my twenty-ninth birthday, I reflected on my life choices and decided I wanted to make new decisions and surrender my ways to God. I said a simple prayer, asking God to take sin from me that I no longer wanted in my life and to deliver me from it. I needed to allow God to lead me in a new direction—toward forgiveness. I had never wished to retaliate or harm anyone for being a perpetrator of pain or sadness in my life. I sought to be a lover and a peacemaker, and no longer wanted to be misunderstood.

My friends explained how my ways affected my relationship with them, and I no longer desired to live in anger. I was tired of being a hypocrite and living a double life, and I no longer wanted to find someone to blame. I desired to go to church, but I lacked trust in people due to my unforgiveness. I wanted to let down guards I had put up out of anger and disappointment at seeing others persevere in ministry while my life had taken a turn for the worse emotionally and spiritually. I was sick and tired; unable to live in freedom from depression, shame, and guilt; and was now facing up to what three years of marriage had showed me—I also dealt with infertility.

Humble yourselves, therefore, under God's mighty hand, that he may lift you up in due time. Cast all your anxiety on him because he cares for you.
1 Peter 5:6–7 NIV

The point of no return was near to me as I reached utter disappointment with my own choices and couldn't settle with the thought that I just might end up alone after all. I reached out to my friend Michelle in Virginia who had known me since we lived in Germany and confessed to her that things that had happened during high school, in church, and with family causing pain and anger. I no longer wanted to keep them bottled up. I wanted to take the step toward forgiveness that I had avoided for eleven years.

She supported my decision and prayed for me so that I could make the call. I reached out to the individual whom I believed needed to know my heart's position on repentance and forgiveness toward him, toward myself, and toward God. When he answered, I began to speak to him about my convictions of repentance and need for forgiveness. I told him everything that had happened to me since we had spoken last, in 2008. It wasn't important to me that he express his regret or remorse for anything that happened. I just wanted to let go of the resentment and bitterness in my heart. I told him that I was forgiving him because I didn't want him to ever think he didn't have an opportunity to repent or ask me for forgiveness. I wanted him to have a prosperous life with his family and the desire to be obedient. My Spirit knew that it was time, it was correct, and it would bring peace.

Bearing with one another and, if one has a complaint against another, forgiving each other; as the Lord has forgiven you, so you also must forgive.
Colossians 3:13 ESV

How could I ask God for forgiveness of that which I was unwilling to forgive and live with for so many years, I thought. After confessing that I had been angry with the results of my choices and deeply resentful as I watched his life as a minister progress over the years, I acknowledged that the unforgiveness in my heart was not hurting him, it was hurting me and leaving me void of Christ. During that time of reflection and conversation, I admitted that I believed that I was unable to conceive during my first marriage because of my past sins and because God was punishing me.

He told me, "Boty, in the Bible there wasn't one barren woman that didn't end up receiving the miraculous gift of a child according to God's will through her faith and prayer." Why the same prophet who was instrumental in robbing me from a hopeful future of love, a family, and ministry was ironically instrumental in speaking words of hope into my new life, I cannot tell you. Some mysteries are only for God to know. But I hoped to live a better life from that point forward. All I remember was feeling relieved and loosed from the bondage of unforgiveness in my past.

Get rid of all bitterness, rage and anger, brawling and slander, along with every form of malice. Be kind and compassionate to one another, forgiving each other, just as in Christ God forgave you.
Ephesians 4:31–32

Weight lifted from me and a new sense of hope was born. I was nowhere near who I am today, but I was on my way to discovering the next layers of deliverance and healing in the forefront. Before my first marriage, my parents knew about my past but did not want to hear the details about what had occurred. I would always come to terms with our differences over the phone or by way of Facebook Messenger. I was compelled to call my parents to tell them I chose to forgive him and let the past go.

"Be angry, and do not sin": do not let the sun go down on your wrath.
Ephesians 4:26

SECTION TWO
A Broken Clay Pot

CHAPTER SIX

Category Three Hurricane

At mealtime Boaz said to her, 'Come over here. Have some bread and dip it in the wine vinegar." When she sat down with the harvesters, he offered her some roasted grain. She ate all she wanted and had some left.

Ruth 2:14 NIV

In May of 2015, I decided to move back into my original apartment in Davie, Florida. My brother and I agreed to not end the lease term so that I could return and spend some time there to myself. Although I enjoyed my own company, I also questioned if I could ever be in a relationship again. I liked having friends and being independent, but also wanted to live a life with purpose and testimony. No longer did I want to live a drama-filled lifestyle in my heart and mind. I was conflicted between my career goals and relationship goals and was once again dreaming about the military. That desire simply wouldn't leave me.

During a virtual meeting at work, I began daydreaming about meeting Mr. Right. Though I don't suggest anyone do this while at work, I fortunately had a cool boss. He and I were scribbling out a game plan for my love life on paper, and he was making sure I didn't leave out my professional goals (desired income and my doctoral degree). I never knew that I could call those things that were not as though they ought to be until I did. I told my boss I was going to meet Mr. Right somewhere on the turnpike sometime in July on my way to my parents' house for a weekend, convinced our meeting would be sudden.

While scrolling on Facebook, I reached out to my friend Don to wish him a happy birthday. We had previously met during my brother's tour in the Marine Corps, and something about him said he would listen and understand me. After I wished him a happy birthday, we continued chatting. I shared my thoughts about wanting to change scenery and do something different. He advised me, "Don't close one door without having another one open." I told him, "I think I want to join the United States Air Force Reserves." He was thrilled with my idea and supported me. I asked, "My dad and my brother don't know, but what do you think?" I was confident we would have more conversations over good cup of *café con leche* or a *cortadito*, depending on the occasion.

> *A wise man will hear and increase learning,*
> *and a man of understanding will attain wise counsel.*
> *Proverbs 1:5–6*

I carried on with my normal busy routine of working at NSU, along with working part-time at Ann Taylor Loft. I'd never had a job in retail before and enjoyed the perks of shopping for my work clothing around the corner from my regular job. I also took up CrossFit training with my cousin Julissa. It was my best way of coping with some of the solitude I felt as I waited on God's direction.

I still had doubts that anyone could love me after knowing my past and my weaknesses, but I believed God knew what was reserved for me. I resumed Bible study with my realtor friend Brandon. When I first met him, he had told me I was like a category three hurricane and that I needed a palm tree in my life for the winds caused.

As we cooked a meal for the homeless ministry at his church, Brandon asked me if I had reconsidered my thoughts on marriage and family. I was already thinking differently about love and shared with him that I desired for God to bless me with someone who loved God so much that he would have no other choice but to love me. I included two other requests, that they be cultured, and to not have crazy loads of unmanageable debt.

Brandon said, "Jo-Jo, he will be of the African persuasion, just not as dark as me. He will love your family very much. He will love God, but he will have a different approach, which is a good thing, because you like a good challenge."

The next day, I realized my life would change forever as I discovered who this man was and how close he was to me. He was nothing like the palm tree Brandon had suggested, he was more like an oak tree, planted. While visiting with my parents at my brother's house in Palm Beach, a few miles north on Florida's turnpike, my brother's wife at the time asked, "Have you considered Don?" I said, "I believe that may be a possibility." Don was supposed to visit my brother that same weekend, and since he didn't, I decided to reach out to him and ask what he ended up doing for his birthday.

The beauty of our conversations evolved as we found more things in common with one another. Despite our opposite backgrounds but similar values in faith, I knew I was safe. Don valued my family, he told me that he knew my brother would be happy with us because Don would take care of me, and he knew that he didn't have to worry about me. The trust wasn't hard to establish, our friendship grew, and we both loved *café con leche*.

Delight yourself in the Lord, and he will give you the desires of your heart.
Psalms 34:4 ESV

I discovered God's love was real. Don was open with me about his past and showed me, through his testimony, how good God truly is. I didn't know love still existed until he came into my life. Some of my friends told me, "Boty, he looks like your dad." He reminded me somewhat of my dad. But why was it so easy to accept Don and love him, since he reminded me of my dad, but I couldn't show my dad the same love and admiration? Don told me, "You'll learn to love your dad because of me."

One week after Don and I got together, he said, "Honeymoon is over!" He wasn't lying. Don wasn't a romantic guy who bought me chocolates and flowers and surprised me at work. Not at the beginning at least. He was more about discipline and minding his own business. It was time for my character to be tested. I was used to being independent and thinking only about myself. This was my first relationship that demanded maturity, discipline, and change.

Clarity and closure on many things about my past weren't arriving soon enough. It would take more tests to prove that to be a real possibility in my heart. I was under the impression I did love. Each time I recollected an experience that formed my thoughts and patterns, another layer was peeled, and more past experiences were brought to memory. It was then that I realized a desire for deliverance would have to become a priority for me.

Both of us were going through a healing process, but most of the time I wanted to focus on his and how it could affect me. I was selfish when it came to relationship goals. After all, I thought, *If this doesn't work out, nothing will ever work for me.* I needed the affirmation and security that I wasn't going to fail one more time at love. I began spending much-needed time in the secret place where I could seek God's love and hope for a future.

"But when you pray, go into your room, close the door and pray to your Father, who is unseen. Then your Father, who sees what is done in secret, will reward you."
Matthew 6:6 NIV

While the honeymoon phase was over and I was dealing with so many emotions, I attempted to throw everything overboard and give up on having a relationship, but Don wasn't one to yield to my emotions. When I exclaimed, "I wish I didn't feel anything!" he told me to be careful not to ask the Lord to grant that. He valued my ways but emphasized the importance of discipline and self-control. I would watch him read Scripture and loved the truth he lived in.

But the fruit of the Spirit is love, joy, peace, forbearance, kindness, goodness,
faithfulness, gentleness and self-control. Against such things there is no law.
Galatians 5:22–24 NIV

He would tell me that we spoke different languages, and he would ask me about my faith. "Who are you?" he would ask. "I hear who you say you are, but who are you?" Later I understood that healing from rejection, understanding the damage it had caused in my life, revealed what Don could see in me. Don, being very discerning, would tell me that who I was, was hidden behind many vain ideas and patterns I was displaying in my behaviors. It was not uncommon for people to tell me I would become the person I did not want to be in my attempt to please people.

Identity and role playing are not the same thing. I was hiding behind intimidation, insecurity, fear, and negative self-talk, but most of all trying to get attention the wrong way. My behaviors resonated with Don's knowledge of manipulation and witchcraft. He would tell me to pray and cast those things into the desert to never return. But in my mind, that couldn't be me who he was talking about until I searched deeper and understood. Nonetheless, he was always my friend and someone I could talk to no matter how frustrating conversations felt. As things progressed in our communication and respect was emphasized, Don assured me that we were equally yoked and God would bless our union.

Do not be yoked together with unbelievers. For what do righteousness and wickedness
have in common? Or what fellowship can light have with darkness?
2 Corinthians 6:14 NIV

Dear God, show me your love. Keep me protected. Continue to use me for your glory. Don't allow those negative spirits to change my love and my compassion for him or others. Please protect my heart. Please make things clear. Please show me your presence. Please, please, I implore and beg you to deliver me from evil and harm. Please free me from my own worst enemies. Please relieve me. Please, in

Jesus's name I pray. Amen.

Infertile

Before leaving Virginia in 2013, I had been diagnosed with polycystic ovarian syndrome (PCOS). When I first arrived in Florida, I consulted with a doctor who conducted some studies and told me I would have a five percent chance of becoming pregnant without fertility treatment. I was not attempting to become pregnant. In fact, I was single. I just wanted to understand my body more and have a proper diagnosis. In my first marriage, I had been unable to conceive and that prompted me to feel broken, useless, and depressed. I was not sure if I had caused this due to my rebellion and former ways of thinking, but before arriving to Florida, I was determined to achieve a healthier lifestyle.

I never wanted to accept that diagnosis or take any medications to treat the condition, so I exercised, changed my eating habits, and met a target weight goal with great discipline and persistence. Keeping up with my physique and outward appearance was rather easy compared to dealing with my internal emotional and spiritual issues. I refused to take medications because I believed there had to be something wrong with that. I used to declare and profess that if I ever was diagnosed with cancer, I would refuse the chemotherapy. I told my doctors I wouldn't take anything unless it was necessary, dreading the idea of addictive patterns. (I'm not saying that it's wrong to consult with doctors or take medication; I just had an aversion to prescriptions for emotional issues and well-being matters that lifestyle changes could affect positively.)

While working in Miami in 2015, a doctoral student came into my office seeking financial assistance. I noticed he was wearing scrubs and asked him if he was a dentist. He said, "No, I'm a fertility doctor." I happened to be assisting with his financial aid but felt compelled to share about my PCOS.

Meanwhile, I was also sad because I was reconsidering my commitment with Don due to unresolved emotional issues that could not seem to reach their end. I was experiencing panic and overall anxiety and felt emotionally withdrawn from Don. I still felt empty even after becoming engaged to a man I believed was heaven sent. I always denied the possibility of an undiagnosed anxiety disorder, but suddenly began considering psychiatric help. My mom would always tell me, "I think you might have generalized anxiety disorder."

Once I shared my thoughts with Dr. Infante, he responded, "You will be fine. I'll bring you more information so you can come to my practice, and we'll address all of your concerns. You'll see that God will heal you and you'll be able to have a child."

"Sing, O barren one, who did not bear; break forth into singing and cry aloud, you who have not been in labor! For the children of the desolate one will be more than the children of her who is married," says the Lord.
Isaiah 54:1 ESV

My Prayer Journal: August 27, 2015

Dear God,

Please talk to my heart. Please tell me you're looking out for me and helping me through this. Dear Lord, please forgive me for acting childish toward myself, my family, and Don. Please allow me another chance to prove that I am willing. Please allow me to show my love through you and to yield to positive outcomes. You know that I wanted this and that everything I have is because it pleases you.

Dear God, please remove all the negative influences and the selfish desires of people. You blessed me with a caring and giving person who has done everything in his power and strength to keep marching forward. Please, Lord, speak to him and show him my sincere heart. I want another chance with Don, and I'm willing to get professional help. Lord, you have seen me through a lot, through it all. You have protected me, guided me, and given me your love and forgiveness despite all my shortcomings.

Dear God, please give me a chance with love again. I vow to make every effort to get closer to you. Please do not take Don away from me. Please help us grow stronger. Please guide us, please protect our relationship. Please bless us with your anointing. Please, Lord, grant us the peace, the joy, the tolerance, and patience.

Please protect our hearts and guard us from all the negative forces that want to destroy us. Lord, I pray this in Jesus's name, amen.

Just as you cannot understand the path of the wind or the mystery of a tiny baby growing in its mother's womb, so you cannot understand the activity of God, who does all things.
Ecclesiastes, 11:5 NLT

Touched by and Angel

Shortly after telling Don that I wanted to reconsider our relationship and our communication, I asked him, "If it could take us two or more years to figure out things would not work with other people, how could we be so sure our relationship was over after a few months?" He was calm and collected all the time. I could barely stand myself because I was full of energy from training at CrossFit and vibrant with health like I had never felt before.

It was a Monday morning back in the office when I prayed and asked God for one more thing. I wanted to know if He really forgave me for my past. I said, "If becoming a mother will be purposeful and this is how you want to show me that you love me, I confess that I would love to have a baby and raise him up to live his life entirely for you." I felt a butterfly flutter in my belly at that very moment. I prayed and asked God to have His way in my life. I felt His forgiveness become evident in my life, and I felt peace.

You might ask, "How could you consider such a petition when you were not married?" During my time at college, I compromised my values and beliefs for what was fitting from the perspective of making sin legal. After personally experiencing the implications, the consequences, the pain, and knowing that the wages of sin is death, I changed my mind about a lot of things. But I was still going through a process of change step by step, and Don and I were nowhere near who we are today.

I understood there was probable cause for my entire family to judge me. I was always afraid of being rejected from family, church, or even society for having a child out of wedlock but God's mysterious way of turning things out for the better helped my faith and conviction to pray for a hopeful future. It wasn't a matter of question for me as to how I could become pregnant suddenly when I'd struggled with PCOS, weight gain, depression, and infertility without even knowing it for many years. But I had enough faith in God that He got my attention when my body was suddenly healed, and it must have been by grace that I could even conceive a child because I knew scientifically it was impossible. In fact, I did not expect to be able to live a life of sin but free of consequences either. But I was convinced of God's evidence in my life for once.

God does things in decency and order. The devil is the father of lies and he seeks to destroy our ability to multiply as women. Hence why I even believed at one point, if my body is not working, then becoming a mother must not be in the cards for me. I even believed in superstition, in fate, and what the enemy's messengers said to me, things that brought doubt, confusion, and eventually deception. And to that I also say, never waste your time on horoscopes, signs, and wonders from astrologers, or even tarot cards. It is all witchcraft, and it is wrong. We walk by faith not by sight and listening to the trap of the enemy on how we should live our life is one of his biggest schemes he uses to get us wrapped up in emotional bondage. Let God's light direct your path, as the Bible says, "Your word is a lamp to guide my feet and a light for my path. Psalm 119:105 (NLT)

Not forgetting the story of Eve in the Garden of Eden in Genesis 3 and so the Enemy continues with whoever decides to listen to his ever-increasing agenda to steal, kill, and destroy. What started with name-calling, turns into our identity, resulting in sinning, which inflicts internal sorrow and pain only God can take away through Christ. But don't be so willing to flirt with sin. Satan will never seek to restore you when you change your mind and only by God's mercy can we know that. It is with this same revelation that I seek for others to understand the same word I have received in Hebrews 10:26, "*Dear Friends, if we deliberately continue sinning after we have received the knowledge of truth, there is no longer any sacrifice that will cover these sins.*" (NLT)

I believed I could not have children unless I chose to seek understanding after my first marriage. I felt condemned for my mistakes and believed God was punishing me from my past when I could not get pregnant. I confess, during the heated fights with my ex-husband when I could not get pregnant, we would fight about terrible things in each other's past. I would shout things one should never shout when angry. The word of God says, "The tongue can bring death or life; those who love to talk will reap the consequences." Proverbs 18:21, NLT. In a chapter later in my story, I will explain further why we must guard our hearts and tame our tongue. The truth remains, having a child would not be with him and that was no mistake in God's hands.

I would never suggest you end a pregnancy or give up a child on the premise of an unplanned pregnancy. A child is a gift from God and the birth of a child will inevitably change your life for the better if you trust in God with all your heart, mind, and soul. If this has been the case in your life, it is not too late to repent and ask God for divine healing, restoration, and cleansing. Let nothing of your past distract your thoughts and rob you from the peace God can restore in your life. I say this to anyone who battles with the deceptive thoughts of unforgiveness. I declare healing and life in your womb in Jesus' name.

Now looking back on this, I realized it was a full-circle moment because not only was this inconceivable during my first marriage, but the date of conception erased the first wedding date that kept appearing on my watch and microwave clock, 8:09. These days I only see 8:28, which reminds me of Romans 8:28: "And we know that all things work together for good to those who love God, to those who are the called according to His purpose."

Dr. Infante was an angel from heaven, and I never even had to go to his office. He showed up at mine. A child is a blessing from heaven, and this baby was the evidence of God's healing touch in my life. Never mistake your choices and consequences with a mistake from God or the wrong idea that He is not in control and He is in the matter. "Every good gift and every perfect gift is from above, and comes down from the Father of lights, with whom there is no variation or shadow of turning" (James 1:17).

The morning after confirming my pregnancy, Don sent me a text on my way to work: *What if we name him Danilo?* The Hebrew form of Danilo means "God is my judge." I called my parents the day I confirmed my pregnancy and I asked if her and dad were sitting down. I asked, "Do you believe in miracles?" They both answered, "Yes!" I shared the news that I was pregnant, and my mom responded in Spanish, "You're pregnant? What are you going to do now? Are you going to get married?" This was followed by my grandmother's similar questioning over the phone from Puerto Rico, and this prompted me to begin praying for the right course of action. Of course, I wanted to be married in the eyes of God, my parents, the church, and the courts.

Upon my family's reaction, I was immediately hit with doubt, guilt, rejection, and fear all at once. After all, I had tried doing everything by the book once before and failed, and the shame and guilt from my past returned to me. I prayed for direction, and I would visit my local church and receive the word that I believed was nourishing and strengthening my faith. I repented for sinning, but I did not have regret for following the path that led me to Don and eventually my pregnancy with Danilo.

But I still struggled with a need to justify everything I ever did wrong. Don't get me wrong, my dad told me when Don and I got together, "Behave." I was already referring to myself as the black sheep of the family. Once again, I was not doing what I thought my parents would want me to do.

Perhaps you have heard of the woman caught in adultery—the one they speak of so often—but never is there mention of the man involved in the story. Well, in this story, it is not specific to those involved but rather what motive was in the hearts of those questioning. Was it condemnation, religion, persecution, or control? Today I understand that Jesus knelt in the dirt, as he did in John 8 for the adulterous woman being accused, and as He wrote who I am, he also raised me up from the dirt and showed me that my sin was forgiven and no longer a slave to the sexual sin of my past.

They were trying to trap him into saying something they could use against him, but Jesus stooped down and wrote in the dust with his finger. They kept demanding an

answer, so he stood up again and said, "All right, but let the one who has never sinned
throw the first stone!" Then
he stooped down again and wrote in the dust. When the accusers heard this, they
slipped away one by one, beginning with the oldest, until only Jesus was left in the
middle of the crowd with the woman. Then Jesus stood up again and said to the
woman, "Where are your accusers? Didn't even one of them condemn you?" "No,
Lord," she said. And Jesus said, "Neither do I. Go and sin no more."
John 8:8–11 NLT

In Thanksgiving in 2015, our family gathered in Alabama and Don and I began discussing possibilities of moving closer to family in either Alabama or Texas. Don began experiencing sadness because of the distance between him and his brothers in Texas, and I was feeling the pressure to prove to myself that I could handle another adjustment without falling apart emotionally. We decided to relocate to his hometown near Houston, Texas. I turned down offers for interviews for higher-paying positions in financial aid at both Miami Dade College and Broward College, attempting to convince myself that it was time to close the chapter in Florida.

Fortunately, I was called for an interview with Houston Community College (HCC) and decided to take a leap of faith and move across the country with Don, hoping the Lord's plans for our lives were better than our own. From the moment we arrived in Texas, we began to get settled into a new space. The only moment I dared to speak about breaking up, Don exclaimed, "Say something stupid again!" Don and I had a different outlook on marriage, and in his eyes, we were married because of his understanding of Texas's common law marriage. The conversations Don and I have always point out the direction he was trying to go, forward, while I was always looking backward with doubt and fear. Yet, he would always help me see things through the lens of faith and without emotional confusion. Don remained direct and assertive in his approach toward working out details for our well-being and never wanted to dissolve our relationship when we faced challenges. His emotional intelligence always challenged me to look past what appeared uncertain because he did not yield to problems, he only sought wisdom from the Holy Spirit. The same month that we arrived in Texas and I began my job at HCC, on a two-hour daily commute to work in Houston traffic while I had a baby on the way, it dawned on us that we missed South Florida and should have never left. Though it may seem silly, it was shortly after getting situated in our apartment near Houston when the adjustment aches and pains began and we both instantly missed Florida. We called my parents and told them we would rather go back to Florida if we could. Dad told us, "Just come this way, stay with us, and figure it out from here." We felt that my parents meant well and were supportive, and I did what I had never done before: resigned from a job with only a moment's notice.

The last thing I imagined was that I would have to face a time of my life that I had left behind not once but twice before, living under my parents' roof. My tests were getting more challenging. I would need to go through a period of testing in order to overcome my past hurts and heal. I never liked doing things without my parent's blessing.

While in Alabama, Don and I visited a church with my parents a few times. On one of those occasions, Don told me, "I will marry you." We spent the duration of my maternity seeking God's will, reading Scripture, and getting to know each other better. At first, he told me, "I don't want to marry you because you're pregnant. I want to marry you because I want to spend the rest of my life with you. Otherwise, once our child grows up, what would be the point?"

But when we arrived at my parent's house, we had a different perspective about how things could be. We read *A Divine Revelation of Hell* by Mary Baxter, which opened us to a different way of seeing things regarding our convictions. I understood and began praying more than ever for God to bless our relationship and our plans to do His will. God would never let me run again, not from His calling for my soul. Moving forward with Don was a fulfillment of my longing desire to have a strong connection to a man of God, and we were strengthening our faith and desire to seek God's instruction as we reached a life-changing event such as parenthood.

My parents told us that some of our church friends from Germany invited us to their church anniversary in Columbus, Georgia, where El Trovador Javier

Rodriguez would be ministering. For the first time since we left Germany in 2000, my family was together at a church gathering that felt familiar and right. During the altar call, I was compelled to go up front and pray. El Trovador approached me the same way he had done in Germany when I was fourteen, except now I was twenty-nine years old. He said, "This is what the Lord says, I have given you what you asked me for. Now return to me your talent."

It was in that moment I knew I could not ask for more. I was carrying a miracle child in my womb that was scientifically impossible, and I had Don. I sincerely sought God's will for my life in marriage, ministry, and family.

He also said, "Show him love," while pointing in Don's direction. Don was not moved to go up front, but my dad persisted to take him up front next to me. That was a day I'll never forget. My soul felt right with the Lord, and I was blessed to understand that there was a purpose in everything and that only God could carry me through a deeper healing process if I was obedient to His instruction.

CHAPTER SEVEN

Unsettled

And so, dear friends, while you are waiting for these things to happen, make every effort to be found living peaceful lives that are pure and blameless in his sight. And remember, our Lord's patience gives people time to be saved. This is what our beloved brother Paul also wrote to you with the wisdom God gave him— speaking of these things in all of his letters. Some of his comments are hard to understand, and those who are ignorant and unstable have twisted his letters to mean something quite different, just as they do with other parts of Scripture. And this will result in their destruction. You already know these things, dear friends. So be on guard; then you will not be carried away by the errors of these wicked people and lose your own secure footing. Rather, you must grow in the grace and knowledge of our Lord and Savior Jesus Christ. All glory to him, both now and forever! Amen.

2 Peter 3:14–18 NLT

Pregnant

Within three months of my delivery date, chaos, confusion, and turmoil arose due to a series of decisions my entire family was making simultaneously. More specifically, my parents, my brother, Don, and me. I was beginning to feel the pressure of moving away yet again. I had transitioned from my doctor in Florida, who had come highly recommended by my former boss's wife, to a doctor in Texas, to my mom's doctor in Dothan, within seven months. I was diagnosed with gestational diabetes and anticipating an unsettling transition as Don would have to return for three weeks to one of the most dangerous jobs I know to be—a boiler maker at a refinery in Texas. Meanwhile, my mom and two of my cousins planned for my baby shower.

I was grateful that in a matter of days after arriving in Dothan, I was able to secure medical insurance and welfare, unaware of the time it would take to obtain employment. My mom would tell me about her difficulties during the time she was pregnant with my brother and me. Her recollection of bad memories during her two pregnancies, "though miraculous," would leave me feeling empathetic. I was always trying to help her see the bright side, and it was as if we had spent just enough time in their home to discover the reality that my parents had hidden from me—who they really were after my brother and I moved out. Mom would apologize after airing out her sadness to Don and me. I just wanted everyone to look on the bright side.

Dothan is a known city in the Bible (Genesis 37:17) in connection with the history of Joseph, as the place in which the sons of Jacob had moved their sheep and, at the suggestion of Judah, the brothers sold Joseph to the Ishmaelite merchants. In my case I had been in transition from one spiritual place since my teen years heading to another twelve years later in hopes of continuing a long-awaited healing journey in the midst of a growing miracle, the birth of our child. Little did I know this was the beginning of discovering the thin line between hope and anguish, emotional bondage, and liberty.

While we were in transition, my parents considered purchasing a larger home and leaving us with their current one at the time. Suddenly, they would be selling the home and we were all moving into the larger home. I still recall the tension and uncertainty that was ever increasing within me, knowing that it was not a good decision for them to make under pressure.

On the day of my baby shower, my dad spent the day at home watching

TV after having a dispute with my mom. Mom left the house to spend the day telling Don and I about it. Later that night, Dad showed up to the baby shower and decided it was a good idea to ask my cousin to bake an additional cake and surprise my mom for her birthday in the middle of the baby shower. It was a bit imprudent and upsetting.

That same night, when all was said and done, Dad kept asking me, "Are we leaving yet?" This has always been what he does when something is not of interest to him. I snapped at him, "Not yet, but if you want to leave, then leave." When we got home, he stopped me on my way to the bedroom and sternly said, "Joanette, let that be the last time." I interrupted, "That what? Are you going to hit me? I am so tired of you treating everyone the way you do, the way you treat Mom, me, etc."

Don walked in between Dad and I, making his presence known. After that moment, nothing else was said. I knew I was no longer that little girl being intimidated by my dad's roaring voice when he became disgruntled. Don and I almost spent the last days before I went into labor in a hotel out in town. I was convinced I didn't want to remain in Alabama. On one hand, everything seemed to be under control, but on the other, we were constantly putting out fires. We spent the week before labor moving into the larger house, and the house we were staying in was sold.

Over some ice cream, I attempted to have a conversation with my parents about my gratitude toward them for everything they had done my entire life. I asked them to consider whether they were happy about their life in general and their relationship with my grandparents in Puerto Rico. For years, we had not traveled there as a family, let alone demonstrated interest in being a part of their life on the island. I didn't want to teach Danilo that this was okay. I questioned how my parents felt about their parents and why they were ok with the separation for so many years. I understood the obvious factors from being raised in a military lifestyle, but I felt that there was a bigger reason I did not understand for distance over time.

I wanted to understand my parents outlook on love, compassion, and relationship with family as we became a bigger family with the arrival of their first grandchild. I wanted my parents to know that they did the best they could, but I still wanted to know what my life would have been like without all the tangible things, the education, and the opportunities their careers afforded us, would love prevail if things were different? Would there be a closer bond between them, my grandparents, their grandchildren.

I really thought it was as easy as talking about feelings, hopes, and dreams. Dad told me, "I always wanted to be like those hero dads." I was at a loss for words. I wanted things to be different at the arrival of his first grandson. My mom was reluctant to hear me out. She just said, "Well, I'm sorry." She had been weighed down with high-strung feelings of disillusionment and just wanted to shower us with gifts as we welcomed baby Danilo.

Wife

The birth of our son, Danilo, changed my life. That moment marked the beginning of a new stage of discovery I could've never prepared for. I wanted to talk about my desire for healing and restoration with everyone in my family, but the time was not opportune. My brother had left for Colombia on a moment's notice a few months prior and returned days before I went into labor. Don was slowly integrating into our family. I felt a sense of neglect for some of the more critical things going on such as my *abuelo's* latest diagnosis and need for dialysis and everyone's mental, emotional, and spiritual health spiraling out of control.

Within a few weeks of my entire family moving into a larger house, things continued to get worse. My mom had been telling me about her frustrations in marriage, ministry, and career since our time working together at the Pentagon in 2007. When she finally blew up, saying things to my dad she would later regret, she came to the room I slept in and told me the things she said to my dad.

I knew this wasn't okay. With so much going on around me, I couldn't find the peace that I needed to end the cycle of pain. I was taking care of our newborn son, learning how to cope with retired disabled veterans, and seeking a way out of dysfunction as quick and as best as I knew how. I was experiencing tremendous discomfort once again because of the conflict between my parents in their home. Suddenly, in a moment of anger, I yelled at my mom that if she didn't hurry up and go to Puerto Rico to tend to my grandmother (her mother), and my dad didn't do that same for his parents, they would one day regret it. The build-up from having attempted so many times to talk about things intensified, and I rebuked my mom. My brother came out of the room he was staying in, asking what happened, and I snapped at him too.

Later, I wrote them both a letter. I am confident to this day, my apologies, my words, and my intent were not well received. My sensitivity to everything around me kicked into overdrive, and I had an intense desire to return to South Florida. Don told me, "I told God the only way I'd marry you is in Florida.

I am not sorry that I sent that severe letter to you, though I was sorry at first, for I know it was painful to you for a little while. Now I am glad I sent it, not because it hurt you, but because the pain caused you to repent and change your ways. It was the kind of sorrow God wants his people to have, so you were not harmed by us in any way. For the kind of sorrow God wants us to experience leads us away from sin and results in salvation. There's no regret for that kind of sorrow. But worldly sorrow, which lacks repentance, results in spiritual death.
2 Corinthians 7:8–10 NLT

Caregiver

On May 28, 2016, we celebrated our marriage ceremony in Marianna, Florida, and began our plans for relocating back to Davie, Florida. Upon arriving there, on welfare and unemployed, I struggled with my pride and doubted how much more God was willing to do for me. At this point, I didn't believe I was doing as much as I could to progress financially and emotionally let alone spiritually. How could we have left and made it back to Florida in one piece, if not by God's grace and mercy?

Feelings of resentment and remorse were on the rise, and I was on the cusp of undiagnosed postpartum depression. My weight fluctuated, and fear, insecurity, and doubt consumed my mind. It was a place of shame I believe many people deal with silently.

No matter how much my husband encouraged me to take walks on the beach, no matter how many Netflix shows we binged on, the only thing I could think was, *How did we end up back at square one?* I struggled to recognize how my selfish, spoiled, high-expectation, unreasonable bouts of depression and frustration with myself hurt my husband and our communication. I didn't realize the Enemy wanted to whisper doubt and fear in my ear and tempt me to give up.

"Not that I was ever in need, for I have learned how to be content with whatever I have. I know how to live on almost nothing or with everything. I have learned the secret of living in every situation, whether it is with a full stomach or empty, with plenty or little."
Philippians 4:11–13 NLT

In my mind, I wanted to be super mom, super wife, and super me. I was convinced I needed a makeover, and I was willing to entertain the idea until reality set in. I became a caregiver, and the Department of Veteran Affairs did not expect me to be a perfect caregiver, just one who cared for my veteran the way he cared for us when he served our country. That came with challenges of getting to know someone else's needs over my own, along with a path of discipline as we would juggle multiple health concerns, routine activities, and growing pains of a new marriage with a baby.

When Danilo was six months old, Don had a total right hip replacement, and I was consumed with complaints and frustration.

The Enemy whispered the most awful things that no one who has been divorced wants to hear a second time in their life. I was convinced that we couldn't come to agreement on anything we talked about. I was still dealing with emotional bondage, and the Enemy knew when we were not aligned in spirit. I would feel frustrated and think I might as well be out of the picture, but Don wouldn't give up, and God covered us in His love and mercy.

Giving family a new opportunity to be close to our son during his first year was also in question, as our move out of Alabama was abrupt. Moving beyond the past was part of learning to let go of pain. Fear and confusion consumed me again when I received calls from two community colleges in Alabama for interviews. I didn't know if that was where we were supposed to be. I contradicted myself each time we considered whether going to Alabama was the right thing to do. Eventually, we even began house hunting and considering the purchase of our first home near my parents.

I was certain about one thing: if we returned, I would not be able to tell you the same story today. I had made up my mind that I would choose depression and abandonment if we had to return there. But after several road trips, conversations, and strong disagreements with my husband, it was evident that the process God was carrying me through was only meant to transform me in my ability to become humbly steadfast and confident in the Lord's direction for our lives. The same words my dad would always reiterate in relation to his opposition for moving back to Puerto Rico to live near my grandparents, I would presume were applicable to my family.

The Lord had said to Abram, "Leave your native country, your relatives, and your father's family, and go to the land that I will show you."
Genesis 12:1 NLT

Nostalgic

Linda (meaning pretty) is what *Abuelo* called me. Traveling to Puerto Rico throughout my life was special and full of memories, from living there as a child for a brief time, to emergency trips from Europe on a moment's notice. I even took my best friends from high school on a few occasions. I had my first wedding there with all of my sisters and friends from college.

The best memories I have include soaking up the sun with my aunts and their friends on the sunny beaches; the juicy Cuban mangos that fell onto my grandfather's roof; the *quenepas, café con leche*, and my maternal grandmother's cooking; and meeting family I had never met before; the amazing scenic routes from coast to coast and the mountains and countryside.

The nostalgia of wanting to be there any time I had vacation time saved or just because became a growing constant over the years, and as soon as Danilo was old enough to make the trip with us, we booked our first family flight to the island. I always dreaded when phone calls came from Puerto Rico because I never knew when I would receive the sad news of my grandfather's passing. The worse part of the phone calls was when the caller began asking about other family members. While much of my family like being in each other's business, I never have. I wasn't always prepared to give an account, and I never wanted to cause any pain. My dad would tell me, "Just say hi and tell them everything's fine," but I could sense my grandparents' growing concern, sadness, and loneliness due to all the years we spent living away from them.

I received much advice from my grandparents throughout my life, but the advice that helped me remain on track as best as I knew how was "Go to church, read your Bible, pray, and respect your husband."

But from everlasting to everlasting the Lord's love is with those who fear him, and his righteousness with their children's children.
Psalms 103:17 NIV

My desire to rise above the circumstances, unemployment, and apathy intensified with a visit from my childhood friend Michelle. She came to visit me the weekend that her church from Virginia was celebrating the inauguration of a campus in Sunrise, Florida. I decided to go with her and during the preaching, the speaker said, "Dance and praise while you're in the hallway!"

I heeded her words. I looked at Michelle, and with tears flowing down both of our faces, we knew God had spoken to our hearts. I began to hope for the best, believing that God had not brought Don and I this far to leave us forsaken and abandoned. Although the Enemy wanted to keep me down, the Holy Spirit was interceding for me and not letting me go.

And the Holy Spirit helps us in our weakness. For example, we don't know what God wants us to pray for. But the Holy Spirit prays for us with groanings that cannot be expressed in words. And the Father who knows all hearts knows what the Spirit is saying, for the Spirit pleads for us believers in harmony with God's own will.

Romans 8:26–27 NLT

I decided to revisit the local church I visited for a little while before leaving for Texas and had livestreamed during my time in Alabama. Don told me, "You look beautiful when you get up and just do your thing!" His compassion and support during that time of our lives proved that God had us in the palm of His hands and that our family would overcome the obstacles no matter what our enemies had said. I wasn't prepared to dive into ministry just yet, though, as I lacked self-awareness and what and who I was becoming.

On many occasions, Don and I would go for a drive with our son on the backroads of Southwest Ranches, Florida. One day, we passed by a white gate bearing a sign that read Segadores de Vida Iglesia Cristiana. The next day, I attempted to log on to the church's Facebook page and livestream their service. I watched for a few moments but then turned it off. I could not understand why I did that, but not long after that, something would happen, and I would understand why I was not ready. It was something new, something different, and something I had never heard before, and I knew everything I tried before proved to be ineffective. I needed to learn from my past and move forward with faith in Christ.

Today I understand I was convicted by the Holy Spirit and rescued when I called on the name of Jesus Christ. I would have to be broken from religious thought patterns, idolatry, and the strongholds from my past, and the Enemy had it out for me to remain ignorant to these matters. I was all too familiar with the gospel, but I was filled with doubt, argument, and rebuttal when it came to my beliefs.

Don would tell me that a mutual friend of ours had warned him, "Joanette is never wrong about anything." I can attribute that to the various encounters I had in the past with my dad and my brother in the presence of our friends. But glory to God for raising men and women to preach, teach, minister, intercede, and deliver a message of faith, hope, and restoration that I could not refrain from when my ears became open to listening to the truth. This was the same message apostle Paul would proclaim as he reached the Jews, Gentiles, and Greeks, among others, through his ministry.

His purpose was for the nations to seek after God and perhaps feel their way toward him and find him—though he is not far from any one of us. For in him we live and move and exist. As some of your own poets have said,

We are his offspring." And since this is true, we shouldn't think of God as an idol designed by craftsmen from gold or silver or stone. God overlooked people's ignorance about these things in earlier times, but now he commands everyone everywhere to repent of their sins and turn to him. For he has set a day for judging the world with justice by the man he has appointed, and he proved to everyone who this is by raising him from the dead.

Acts 17:27–30 NLT

SECTION THREE
Back to the Potter's House

CHAPTER EIGHT

Redirected

Trust in the Lord with all your heart and lean not on your own understanding; in all your ways acknowledge Him, and He shall direct your paths.
Proverbs 3:5–6

Saddled Up

In July 2017, after applying to sixty-three jobs all over South Florida, I was offered a position at Palm Beach State College, as the admissions advisor for the bachelor's degree programs. We moved to the world's equestrian capital Wellington, Florida, in Palm Beach County, but first, we celebrated with a road trip victory lap in our new Toyota RAV4 Hybrid to Virginia. I wanted Titi Carmen, Normarie, and Tito to meet Don and Danilo for the first time.

I was eager to get back into the swing of things with work. My boss, Laura, advised me well regarding the politics and culture at the college and trusted in my ability to create my own experience, as my position was new at the college. My Cuban coworker, Milly, would say, *"Estas accabando,"* which translated to English means "you're killin' it!" I enjoyed what I did; it had been a while since I was able to give it my best in the workplace.

Often, Laura would ask, "JR, how is your red?" because she knew I had a short fuse when it came to interpersonal dilemmas. She was helpful and working there reminded me so much of my time at DeVry University, where I worked closely with my boss, Lisa, who also called me JR and mentored me in professional development. I was back in the saddle!

As Hurricanes Harvey and Irma brushed and swept through Texas and Florida, followed by the sweeping of Maria through Puerto Rico, I attempted to remain connected with my family, realizing death could be closer than we ever imagined and it was crucial to grab a hold of those precious moments that could be lost in an instant.

We traveled to and from Alabama, Puerto Rico, and Virginia during vacation time. But as I encountered new opportunities within the education field, I learned about Southeastern University, a Christian university in Lakeland, Florida which offered an online doctoral degree program in organizational leadership. I decided to push restart with what NSU had afforded me in 2014 and I desired to finish.

Crippled

It was Saturday again. "The day after this but the day before that." I had come to realize I had a family, my health, and a career. At my mom's encouragement, I had recently lost forty pounds and felt fabulous physically. I was entertaining the idea of a small business, preparing to take some overdue writing courses, and planning for the next adventure with a total physical transformation.

But I was backsliding, sad, and crying due to lack of understanding my purpose and destiny. But worse, I still did not have my hope and joy restored—only belief and conviction that something would have to change. Though I knew I am a child of God, I did not understand what had crippled me for so many years and I wanted to know. My emotions were waging against my purpose and I knew that it was time to reach a resolution.

I was waiting for Sunday. I needed to hear from God. After watching a series of worship music videos on YouTube by Christine D'Clario, a Christian artist, and her testimony, I ran into a sermon on YouTube from Pastor Ruddy Gracia, "Emotional Warfare," followed by Maria Gracia's documentary, 44. I was brought to tears and challenged to stand up. A sudden impulse and hunger for a deeper sense of purpose returned to me like never before. I sent the video to my dad and to my brother. The words Pastor Ruddy spoke on were resonating within my spirit, and I knew that my family could experience a breakthrough and restoration with just a mustard seed of faith.

"Enter his gates with thanksgiving; go into his courts with praise. Give thanks to him and praise his name."
Psalm 100:4 NLT

On January 21, 2018, I invited my brother, who'd returned to South Florida for work, to the church Don and I had passed on one of our drives one year prior. The one with the white walls bearing the sign "Segadores de Vida Iglesia Cristiana." The sound of the whistles blowing as the parking attendants directed traffic, the hot gravel we walked on to enter the front doors, the smell and feel of the tropical weather, and the multitude of people representing all of Latin America and the Caribbean was comforting, along with the aroma of Cuban coffee from Sega Café, the toasted pastries, and the people serving one another and approaching each detail of the service with enthusiasm and joy.

All of this reminded me of the Salvation Army in Ponce, Puerto Rico, where my grandparents took me on many occasions. It was overwhelming and heart-wrenching at the same time. Today I know that what pulled on me wasn't the culture or the environmental scent but rather the glory and presence of God that filled the atmosphere from the parking lot all the way into the building like no other place I had ever visited before. I knew I wouldn't leave that place the same as when I arrived.

Pastor Ruddy sang "I Surrender All," and later that afternoon, I saw a Facebook Live video of my abuelo singing the same song at the Salvation Army in Puerto Rico. It was not a coincidence that for three years, the Enemy had been putting up a fight for me to never set foot in the Potter's house, for I had found my home and Pastor Ruddy would become the spiritual father I always hoped for. I walked in carrying a load, and I left with a lighter one. I surrendered all.

On a Sabbath Jesus was teaching in one of the synagogues, and a woman was there who had been crippled by a spirit for eighteen years. She was bent over and could not straighten up at all. When Jesus saw her, he called her forward and said to her, "Woman, you are set free from your infirmity." Then he put his hands on her, and immediately she straightened up and praised God. Indignant because Jesus had healed on the Sabbath, the synagogue leader said to the people, "There are six days for work. So come and be healed on those days, not on the Sabbath." The Lord answered him, "You hypocrites! Doesn't each of you on the Sabbath untie your ox or donkey from the stall and lead it out to give it water? Then should not this woman, a daughter of Abraham, whom Satan has kept bound for eighteen long years, be set free on the Sabbath day from what bound her?" When he said this, all his opponents were humiliated, but the people were delighted with all the wonderful things he was doing.
Luke 13:10–17 NLT

As I continued attending SDV, I began learning about faith and grace more than ever before. "So then faith comes by hearing, and hearing by the word of God" (Romans 10:17). Each of us has a mission, and God's divine purpose for our life comes with a manual and a set of rules we must learn and follow if we desire to be authentic, trusted, respected, and followed as leaders in the kingdom. I was tired of stagnation and spiritual lethargy for the past eighteen years of my life. I'd felt the Lord's touch like the woman from Luke 10. I believed the door was open for me.

It was only a matter of time before I would receive "the affirmation" to serve and be a part of this ministry as this call was just as important to me then as it was when I was fourteen. Only this time, I might be doing things in unorthodox ways, something nondenominational, just Christian. I had found the mega church I was looking to get plugged into when I left Alabama in 2014, and I made up my mind even if they called me foolish.

The message of the cross is foolish to those who are headed for destruction! But we who
are being saved know it is the very power of God.
1 Corinthians 1:18 NLT

The Interim

Seven months after starting my job at Palm Beach State College and getting plugged in at SDV, I was convicted to begin giving. Having grown up in ministry, I never doubted the impact of obedience to the Word of God, although very much fearful of the consequences for disobedience. Malachi 3:10 says, "Bring all the tithes into the storehouse, that there may be food in My house, and try Me now in this," says the Lord of hosts, "if I will not open for you the windows of heaven and pour out for you such blessing that there will not be room enough to receive it."

For so many years I heard my parents talk about their faithful giving and never lacking. I knew that I could try this for myself and find out for myself because it wasn't one of my greater conflicts in ministry. I never doubted what sowing into the kingdom meant. I had experienced a different type of robbery in my past. So, for all I knew and believed, being a cheerful giver was simple obedience and reverence.

I was surprised how only a few weeks after beginning to give, on February 12, 2018, I received a call from my college's administration and was invited to discuss an opportunity that quickly turned into an offer for a promotion to interim campus registrar. I was chosen to take on the role due to my experience in financial aid at one of the largest community colleges in the United States, Northern Virginia Community College. My understanding of a campus registrar was that of an administrator for the campus, until the dean of enrollment management services told me, "This position has been treated as a glorified clerk, and you'll need to become a great manager, get the paperwork off your desk, and learn so that you can become a leader."

For it is God who works in you both to will and to do for His good pleasure.
Philippians 2:13

Soon after assuming the role, I became more interested in the maturing process. I finally hung up my degrees in my office ten years after graduation. It was my second opportunity to be a campus leader. I was completely devoted to this new path I was following, with church, career, and family life in West Palm Beach, and I was about to step into a new level of training that I believed I would be able to endure with God on my side. Although I was initially rejected by the team, who said, "You're too young," and "I want my old registrar back," I accepted my new role with enthusiasm.

I had to hire six new staff members. With two in mind already and the other applicants being highly recommended individuals, I collaborated closely with human resources. I was excited to finally dust off my first master's degree! The veteran staff had my full support to train the new employees and receive individualized feedback on their annual reviews, which stunned them. "No one has ever given me this type of annual review," one told me. "I will show my granddaughter when she is all grown up."

The encouragement and empowerment were well received, and the team became grateful for the changes we were making. This process brought a positive morale to the team, and the mission for the department was met with exceptional effort and results from each staff member. By the time we reached one year as a team, our feedback from leadership was positive and motivating.

My supervisor gave me positive feedback and listened to me. I was applauded for my accomplishments. My coworkers and staff would come to my office around the clock just to say hi, to chat, to discuss ideas, or just to vent and leave with some type of encouragement. In times like these, I pondered what it could be like if all higher education institutions offered chaplain services, I would consider this to be a privilege to people with spiritual needs. Meanwhile, I needed wise counsel. I felt loaded and lacking so much wisdom I could only get from praying, reading, and talking to Don about everything. I sought mentorship and connection with other leaders. I wanted to learn more about upholding the integrity of an organization while juggling multiple challenges with staffing and student needs. I wanted to do what was right. Wasn't that the scope of a rule keeper at the institution? I joined multiple working groups on campus and was even deemed cluster chair for the registrar cluster, but my greatest motivation and reward came from going to church every Sunday to learn more about God's strategies and miracles.

Redoma (Earthen Flask)

In May 2018, I attended my first Redoma—SDV's annual women's conference. At Redoma, I fell in love again. I found joy for everything I thought had been lost in the past. It was refreshing to my soul.

> *Therefore my heart is glad and my tongue rejoices;*
> *my body also will rest secure,*
> *because you will not abandon me to the realm of the dead,*
> *nor will you let your faithful one see decay.*
> *You make known to me the path of life;*
> *you will fill me with joy in your presence,*
> *with eternal pleasures at your right hand.*
> *Psalm 16:9–11 NIV*

The theme was "joy," and Pastor Ruddy said, "Redoma has been a trampoline for many women and their families in restoration, direction, business, and ministerial endeavors." Not knowing how far the leap would have to be, I decided to jump for joy! I left filled with joy and hope for a new season in my marriage, my finances, my career, and my ministry. I returned to my home recharged. I still remember the moment I acknowledged my attitude and outlook on life from a place of emotional rejection.

One of the most memorable segments was Pastor Yesenia Then's among other topics for thousands of women that weekend. She preached about Leah in Genesis 29, and it was the first time I began to reckon with my own ways and my desire to change my behavior as a woman of God. How could I be an inspiration to others when I still dealt with these unresolved emotional patterns in my heart?

I was full of resentment and bitterness from childhood through adulthood because I lacked humility and devotion unto God above all things. I had little to no awareness of how self-absorbed I had become and how many of my ways were characterized as manipulative and controlling. I had little to no understanding of how my choices affected those around me. Recognizing my defects would be a long road to change. But the key ingredient was rejoicing and praising as I learned from the story of Leah who suffered rejection, insecurity, and behaved according to her emotions until she traded her lament for worship to God.

When the Lord saw that Leah was hated, he opened her womb, but Rachel was barren. And Leah conceived and bore a son, and she called his name Reuben for she said, "Because the Lord has looked upon my affliction; for now my husband will love me." She conceived again and bore a son, and said, "Because the Lord has heard that I am hated, he has given me this son also." And she called his name Simeon. Again she conceived and bore a son, and said, "Now this time my husband will be attached to me, because I have borne him three sons." Therefore his name was called Levi. And she conceived again and bore a son, and said, "This time I will praise the Lord." Therefore she called his name Judah. Then she ceased bearing.
Genesis 29:30–35 ESV

SDV is a transformational church offering leadership development with an emphasis on small homogeneous cell groups called H.E.C.H.O.S. (Hispanics in Every Home Offering Salvation). Praise the Lord for the intention and desire the Lord had placed in my heart to attend Redoma and connect with others from SDV. I was able to meet Bishop Ruddy Gracia and his daughter Vanessa Gracia Cruz at their book signing and connect with some of the most influential leaders at SDV, who would help mold my growth and development as a Christian.

When I was a child, I spoke as a child, I understood as a child, I thought as a child;
but when I became a man, I put away childish things.
1 Corinthians 13:11 NLT

After Redoma I began reading books that enriched my soul and inspired me to seek more of the Word of God. I started becoming more acquainted with the stories from the Bible. Some of my favorites were the least discussed in my upbringing in the church. Once I decided to take doctoral courses at Southeastern University, I was required to apply a biblical worldview in my course work and realized I needed to spend more time studying the Word of God. I started with a thirty-one-day challenge in the book of Proverbs, the book of wisdom. The next month, July 2018, I started listening to discipleship lessons by Yesenia Then on YouTube on Monday nights. I joined a H.E.C.H.O.S. group and began attending it weekly, which began to challenge my trust in the people God would use to guide, admonish, teach, and lead me through many areas of growth and maturity. The most valuable change came from my leader's fervent prayers and constant reaching out to me. The first time my group leader asked me to pray aloud, I told her, "I'm shy." That wasn't exactly the truth. I wasn't shy to speak; I was shy to pray. My leader told me, "Soon you'll be praying confidently out loud!"

My leader would call me in the mornings on my way to work and some evenings after work. I didn't realize that some of the "church hurt" lingered until my new church sought to engage with me. Colossians 1:28 says, "He is the one we proclaim, admonishing and teaching everyone with all wisdom, so that we may present everyone fully mature in Christ" (NIV). I believed this was the beginning of a divine shift in my home, in my spiritual life, and in my family's life.

Blessed are the poor in spirit, for theirs is the kingdom of heaven.
Blessed are those who mourn, for they will be comforted. Blessed are the meek,
for they will inherit the earth. Blessed are those who hunger and thirst for righteousness,
for the will be filled. Blessed are the merciful, for they will be shown mercy. Blessed are
the pure in heart,

for they will see God. Blessed are the peacemakers, for they will be called children of
God.

Blessed are those who are persecuted because of righteousness, for theirs is the kingdom
of heaven. Blessed are you when people insult you, persecute you and falsely say all
kinds of evil against you because of me. 12 Rejoice and be glad, because great is your
reward in heaven, for in the same way they persecuted the prophets who were before
you." Matthew 5:3–12 (NIV)

Short-Sighted

I considered myself to be built up to my fullest potential with academia and job titles in higher education by age thirty-two, but I felt short with my vague understanding of success. I wanted to inspire and motivate others while I struggled with my own foolish thought patterns. I was not comfortable with monotony or routine. I lost interest in anything that did not yield quick results. My faith wavered. I wanted so much in so little time. I wanted my family to come to church with me, for my team at work to succeed and get promoted, for my personal well-being to remain intact, and I wanted permission to complain anytime I felt like I wanted to. I was being selfish and inpatient. Don said, "Like the Marine Corps would say, 'Good initiative, bad judgment.'"

> *'But seek first the kingdom of God and His righteousness,*
> *and all these things shall be added to you."*
> *Matthew 6:33*

I lacked discipline and endurance, character, and perseverance. As mankind, we are challenged to seek and explore our interest in a trade or have a special talent that relates to our ability to multiply or expand our limited understanding of a purposeful pursuit in life. For Christians, this pursuit is (or should be) driven by faith not by sight, by cultivating the fruits of the Spirit which are love, joy, peace, forbearance, kindness, goodness, faithfulness, gentleness and self-control

(Galatians 5:22). I was far from achieving this because I still struggled with the thought patterns in my mind. If I didn't see what I wanted to see, the job, the house, the material things, the way I wanted them to be, I thought there must be something wrong with me, or something wrong with the other person or the place.

No matter how much my assigned leader from SDV prayed with me and encouraged me, I had a nagging desire to argue, give up, and resist sound advice from Don. I couldn't stand it when he would tell me that I refused to listen because I always remembered how my dad would say I don't listen. Except, Don was trying with so much patience and consideration unto God.

Burnout always made me uncomfortable. I began complaining to Don about my routine by making excuses such as, "I want to work closer to our home, or buy a house and perhaps that might solve the issue," or "Let's just move away and be closer to family." An insurmountable list of ideas ran through my mind, and I could not leave it up to time; I was inpatient. This time it cost my family over ten thousand dollars for making the mistake of almost purchasing a home for the second time. I started wheezing, feeling physical discomfort, and believing that West Palm Beach was the problem. My allergist told me, "You are allergic to palms." That was the last straw. I was becoming allergic to everything in my office, in the village, and to make matters worse, I thought I was too good to be where I was. Talk about vain!

Unless the Lord builds the house, they labor in vain who build the house, but if the Lord builds the house, the destroyers labor in vain.
Psalms 127:1 NLT

Coincidently, I was pursued by another administrator from the college campus conveniently closer to our house and learned from my supervisor that she had requested that I be sent to her campus. My directors refused my request to transfer to the other campus. I never learned how to handle rejection, let alone being told what I wasn't going to do. This would have been the right time to begin the application of all the Word I was hearing and reading.

But don't just listen to God's word. You must do what it says. Otherwise, you are only
fooling yourselves. For if you listen to the word and don't obey, it is like glancing at
your face in a
mirror. You see yourself, walk away, and forget what you look like. But if you look
carefully
into the perfect law that sets you free, and if you do what it says and don't forget what
you heard, then God will bless you for doing it.
James 1:22–25 NLT

I was short-sighted. I instantly became anxious to apply to jobs in Miami, in Lakeland, and in Broward. Where was I going this time? I even decided to transfer from one H.E.C.H.O.S. group to another closer to my house because I questioned everything. What was I really running from? Rather than quitting, I slowly learned it was not all about me, and my move would have to be about God. Opportunities for me to learn and grow appeared as I attended more conferences and listened to the Word of God, but the next challenge was overcoming a mindset of self-righteousness and spending time seeking the presence of God in my home, in my car on my way to work, and everywhere I would go.

My training would be about transformation and authenticity, which would require patient endurance, spending time getting to know who I was, and sacrifice. It is worth mentioning at this point in my story one of the key lessons I discovered early in my search for identity, purpose, and destiny, from one of my favorite authors and preachers of this generation, Yesenia Then.

Because as agents of the Lord, we represent His interests on Earth, and it is precisely God's interest that you identify what He has designed you for and become everything He wanted you to be when He created you. Your internal resources, such as your talents, gifts, and abilities, speak of the form the Lord wanted to give you. The place where you are today, regardless of your present condition) represents the space where He wanted to put you. It would be impossible, for you to have what you have and be where you are, if God wouldn't have allowed it. On this basis, we can know that your Creator has expectations of you. God perfectly knows what you can attain, and He expects you to do it. From *I Challenge You to Grow*:

It was about being where I was supposed to be and doing what I was supposed to be doing. I knew I needed to pick up my cross and follow Christ. The time had come. The work would begin. I sought a new horizon. I wanted to hear the Word of God constantly. I couldn't go to a service without extending an invitation to my friends and family or sending them the link for the livestream. As Hebrews 4:12 says, "the word of God is alive and active. Sharper than any double-edged sword, it penetrates even to dividing soul and spirit, joints and marrow; it judges the thoughts and attitudes of the heart" (NIV).

My mom had always told me, "When you come back, I know you will be radical." She would say, "When you get older, you might become like the American Gospel Singer Judy Jacobs who is also a renowned preacher in our current generation." What a compliment! But honestly, I just wanted to be me and to be refined into who God wanted me to become. I became an avid seeker of mentorship and discipleship. Because of the time I spent away from the church, I felt as if I couldn't get enough Word in my life. My priorities shifted as God filled the hole in my heart that only He could fill.

We can rejoice, too, when we run into problems and trials, for we know that they help us develop endurance. And endurance develops strength of character, and character strengthens our confident hope of salvation. And this hope will not lead to disappointment. For we know how dearly God loves us, because he has given us the Holy Spirit to fill our hearts with his love. Romans 5:3–5 NLT

Repositioned

My new favorite thing to do on Saturday mornings was catch up on sermons and take notes. One Saturday afternoon I was livestreaming a women's conference sponsored by Casa De Amor y Fe in Lakeland, Florida, called *Mujeres de Influencia*. Yesenia Then preached on the Shunammite woman in 2 Kings, whom she also wrote about in *Mujer Reposicionate (Women, Reposition Yourself)* and had preached about at Redoma earlier that year. I must have been in the right places at the right time and God must have been pulling on me with this specific message. I will have to listen to this message again later on my journey.

The Shunammite was a notable woman "worthy of imitating," although her name isn't given in the text. The woman in this story was known for her valor and her reverence for God by taking care of His prophet, and she was recognized for her respect of her husband. In her submission to her husband, she demonstrated what we as the church should be unto Christ as the head of the church, as it says in Colossians 3:18 and Ephesians 5:23. Her self-control is admirable, as she discussed matters only with those appointed by God, which included not bombarding her husband with dilemmas that only she and the prophet needed to discuss (2 King 4:22–28). She made every opportunity count and did not conform to do anything less than the perfect will of God in her life.

This messaged revealed the strategies she would use to hold onto the promise from the words the prophet spoke into her life. As Yesenia Then says, "With the adversity you may be going through today, God is building a testimony that will bring blessing to your tomorrow." I considered this word meaningful to my life because, in that moment, I was reaching for an answer about the next steps my family should take—whether it represented one more move or developing a plan for our future.

I still needed to grow from past experiences and avoid making the same mistakes I had in the past. I acknowledged that I had lived with fear all the years of my life and I desired to change, but I was barely getting started with a walk by faith. We would only move when God indicated it was time. Running was no longer an option, and most importantly, God's promise would not be buried because it was going to be fulfilled in His perfect timing.

Through Don's words, the Holy Spirit reminded me to choose God over my flesh (emotions), to not call His blessings a curse, and to not complain. Not complaining also meant asking God for discernment and not talking about the process or steps with the wrong people. As Yesenia Then says, "Not all people have the maturity to give you word or guidance you need to receive at certain times."

It was then that I began desiring a deeper relationship with God through prayer. In my case, everything was just fine, we had church, a luxurious lifestyle in West Palm Beach. My brother lived next door. What else could I possibly want.

As I continued livestreaming the conference that Saturday afternoon, I became prayerful about the possibility of moving to Lakeland, because Southeastern University is located there, and my husband had enjoyed living in Lakeland when he was stationed there on Temporary orders as a Marine Recruiting Assistant.

Our family in Alabama was a little closer. Don would be slightly closer to Texas and Louisiana, where he had a brother from the Marine Corps. I sensed restoration becoming real, perhaps the dreams I had when I lived in Virginia, which included the possibility of owning a home again. But little did I know as I listened to the Word, these words were not limiting my family to tangible assets or another baby, because we have our son, but a divine purpose.

Call her back again," Elisha told him. When the woman returned, Elisha said to her as she stood in the doorway, 'Next year at this time you will be holding a son in your arms!" "No, my lord!" she cried. "O man of God, don't deceive me and get my hopes up like that."

But sure enough, the woman soon became pregnant. And at that time the following year she had a son, just as Elisha had said."

2 Kings 4:15-17

CHAPTER NINE

Nomad

He had to go through Samaria on the way.
John 4:4 NLT

The Send

In February 2019, I attended The Send at the Camping World Stadium in Orlando, Florida. Lou Engle—an intercessor; visionary; and co-founder of The Call, a prayer and fasting movement responsible for gathering hundreds of thousands around the globe—called for a forty-day fast. Seventeen thousand people committed to joining The Jesus Fast, which would last from March 1, 2019 to April 9, 2019.

In *The Jesus Fast*, Engle states, "I would call the entire planet to a forty-day fast! I am stirred to believe that if we do this, revival will break out everywhere." I spent the duration of the fast reading this book and discovering the relevance between the influence of John the Baptist, events such as the Azusa Street Revival, the multiple prayer and fasting meetings across the United States over the past one hundred years, and the accounts of many dedicated missions and ministers to an ongoing revival.

126

Lou Engle, Daniel Kolenda, Ruddy Gracia, Francis Chan, Todd White, Andy Byrd, Loren Cunningham, Benny Hinn, and Teo Hayashi, among others, led a prayer and worship event that lasted twelve hours, resulting in more than seventy-nine thousand documented decisions to follow Christ and continuing, and a call to the African American, Latino, and Brazilian communities for laborers to go out to the high schools, neighborhoods, universities, and nations. I experienced a new spirit of worship, soul healing, restoration, and equipping like never before in a crowd of over fifty thousand people. Since I was a child, I had yearned to go to the unreached, preach the gospel, and heal the sick.

The Send was a declaration of war on inaction, and I left it ready to go. I will never forget the young man who prayed for me as we declared healing, deliverance, and a sending to the nations. God placed Venezuela, Italy, Europe, the Caribbean, and North America on my heart, and the young man said, "Lord, send her where I can't go in Jesus's name."

Not that I considered going back to live in Mannheim, Germany but I always wondered what it could be like to return to Europe with my family to live and do ministry. I always had fond memories of Germany and Italy and nothing I had ever achieved living in the states could replenish the longing I retain for returning to Europe. I learned that of the many places I traveled to as a child with my family, the significance of history and how it would become relevant in today's social and political challenges would coincide with my desire to be on a mission overseas if ever afforded to me. I wondered, *how can this come to pass Lord.*

I remember the Christian retreats my family went to in places such as Garmisch-Partenkirchen, Berchtesgaden, Neuschwanstein and Amsterdam, Holland just to name some. We used different modes of transportation, trains, planes, and boat rides making photographic memories that to this day cause nostalgia. But to my surprise I learned that in recent years the place of my upbringing measuring 144-acres of land considered to be the largest Army Barracks in Germany would become a Syrian refugee-camp. Benjamin Franklin Village, the military post where my childhood and teen years formed a part of my identity was reduced to a refuge and no longer accessible to the American citizens once residing there since post

World War II era. Like many times in the past, I wondered, *will I ever get to retrace those places and experience the revival we would often pray for in the past.* The post cards, museum brochures, and collection of souvenirs my family still treasures give me contentment for the better times we shared as a family. Telling Don these memories inspire him to want to go someday.

Thirsty

By March 2019, my family had relocated to Central Florida. The place where dreams began to return to me was bittersweet, as I left my church of just one year. It was as if the reboot button was pushed too soon. As my thirty-third birthday approached, I realized that Christ had gone through much more than I had in thirty-three years of life. I also realized that He too had to pass through Samaria.

As my past and present aligned, I learned the original plans God had for me were linked to the times and places of my past. I wouldn't be able to teach a lesson I had yet to learn. There was a cost. Yesenia Then says in *I Challenge You to Grow*, "What are you not doing that you should be able to develop? More than an option, our continuous growth, is the demand that has been established by the Lord that the Lord requires of us."

I read more books in 2018 and 2019 than I had ever in my educational journey. Jesus left examples for me to follow and a responsibility to grow so that I would bear fruit and multiply in others. The highlights of my day were student workers and staff coming into my workspace and spending time talking about their goals, their classes, and what they wanted to do when they graduated college. Nothing gave me more satisfaction than meeting people who hungered for an experience that would change their circumstances and provoke a transformation in their lives.

The fear of the Lord is true wisdom; to forsake evil is real understanding.
Job 28:28 NLT

Hungry

John Ortberg's *Who Is This Man?* reminded me of my roots in education, as well as my ministry calling, college years, positions I had held, and experiences in Rome and growing up in Germany. I wondered, *Was it all in vain? Why did I ever get to have a good life if this was it?* I read about the universities in Rome, Vienna, and Heidelberg—the cities that'd I visited and lived in. The accounts of Jesus's influence in the establishment for those who, according to philosopher Mark Nelson, "have institution of self-giving for the lonely, schools, hospitals, orphanages for those who will never be able to repay" and the roots of Jesus's movement became known to me. I wondered if I would ever get the opportunity to travel to those places again. After all, my desire for pursuing the military had stemmed from a heart to serve in missions.

Command and teach these things. Don't let anyone look down on you because you are young, but set an example for the believers in speech, in conduct, in love, in faith and in purity. Until I come, devote yourself to the public reading of Scripture, to preaching and to teaching. Do not neglect the spiritual gift you received through the prophecy spoken over you when the elders of the church laid their hands on you. Give your complete attention to these matters. Throw yourself into your tasks so that everyone will see your progress. Keep a close watch on how you live and on your teaching. Stay true to what is right for the sake of your own salvation and the salvation of those who hear you.

1 Timothy 4:11–16 NLT

In my thirteen years of working in higher-education admissions and financial aid, I always told students and staff, "They can take your house, your cars, and your possessions, but one thing they can never take away is your education." Training my staff, writing, doing a little public speaking, and dedicating time to school, I thought, *Many things belong to Caesar, but not my calling*. I knew God places people where He wants to glorify Himself through our process and our purpose. In Him I felt able to learn and teach others all He had taught me, to seek Him first. Even still, I had to change my mind and my heart. I was focused on not being able to reach my family and bring them to church with me.

I asked one of the leaders at SDV to pray for me because I was still experiencing frustration and anger. My family did not accept all my invitations, nor did they express the enthusiasm I desired, to go with me to church. She told me after praying, "You have to change your mind. It is not what God will not do; it is something you have to change your mind about." I had negative thought patterns. I would resent spending time with family over going to SDV or other Christian events because I wanted to seek more of the things I was attracted to. I had found a new sense of purpose, to seek God in everything that I was doing. I wanted to talk about Him, and I had a hunger for being a part of ministry full-time.

Quitting my job for full-time ministry was not exactly what God had spoken. It would have to be more about learning to walk with Him in His presence and growing steadfast. I wanted to learn more about the sacred things and consecration, as John the Baptist was portrayed in Scripture. John the Baptist, Daniel, and Jesus Himself understood wilderness. I had yet to learn wilderness lessons. But as I became more uncomfortable with the amount of work, I was responsible without a doubt, but I was feeling void without a true experience like those we learn about in the Bible which take place in the wilderness.

One more thing I recall not being supported for, when I was heading to MBC in 2004 to become a VWIL Cadet in the only all-women cadet corps in the U.S., was that "I would not like being outdoors." Ironically, my spirit man desired this experience so that I could do the work of the Great Commission.

But solid food is for the mature, who by constant use have trained themselves to distinguish good from evil.
Hebrews 5:14 NIV

I couldn't get enough of God's presence in my everyday life. Quite frankly, I wanted to spend all my time praying, reading, and seeking His presence. I wanted to stay as far away from religion as possible, and I became unapologetic about my desires and pushed forward.

In those days John the Baptist came preaching in the wilderness of Judea, Repent, for the kingdom of heaven is at hand. For this is he who was spoken of by the prophet Isaiah when he said, 'The voice of one crying in the wilderness: 'Prepare the way of the Lord; make His paths straight.'"
Matthew 3:13

My group leader advised me to use the time of prayer and fasting in January 2019 with our church to seek God's direction. Prior to culminating with the twenty-one-day corporal fasting and praying, I was offered a permanent position at Polk State College in Lakeland, with an apartment and Danilo's new school lined up. Everything happened so fast it almost felt too good to be true.

It became bittersweet on the days leading up to my departure from Palm Beach State College. I almost changed my mind instantly. My leader told me to not give it too much thought and to focus on God's direction and instruction. It was best to trust in Him in everything that was taking place.

I was certain about the transition being a part of God's divine purpose for our lives and assured that it was time to listen to the prophets more than ever:

"So they rose early in the morning and went out into the Wilderness of Tekoa; and as they went out, Jehoshaphat stood and said, 'Hear me, O Judah and you inhabitants of Jerusalem: Believe in the Lord your God, and you shall be established; believe His prophets, and you shall prosper'" (2 Chronicles 20:20).

On Sunday morning, my favorite day of the week, after recently settling into our apartment in Lakeland, I was livestreaming SDV and became overwhelmed by the presence of the Holy Spirit after asking Him to visit me and let me know that He was with me. Don would remain in West Palm Beach for eight months because we had two lease agreements as a result of our move.

Reunited

Regardless of the distance from Lakeland to Southwest Ranches, I was more than willing to be with the ladies for Girls Night Out at SDV on May 5,

2019. At the event, one of my church sisters from Germany, Yvette, and I reunited after nineteen years. She had been accepting my invitations to services online from Alabama, and upon moving to Florida, sought a new place called home as well, SDV.

The most unimaginable thing happened during our reunion: she told me she was swearing into the United States Air Force Reserves that week. I was surprised and excited because I thought our age exceeded the Reserves limit, but I was wrong. My desire for going into the military stemmed from my upbringing in a military family, living overseas, and working for the Department of Defense. I missed the structure, discipline, order, and security. Having noted the opportunities in my upbringing and blessings that came with being in the government sector, I had always placed this desire on the top of my list of goals and aspirations.

During one of many trips to SDV, the last thing I imagined was the restitution of dreams that were on their way by just daring to believe in the impossible. My bishop had said it during several service altar calls: "Dare to believe what you have never believed, and watch God do what you have never seen Him do." I was inspired because I had experienced many obstacles and realized, *this can't be a coincidence. The obstacles must be purposeful.*

I was taken back to the conversation I had with Don in 2015. I hadn't realized I was always on the path back to my dream, and it dawned on me then—chaplaincy. At Redoma 2019, the theme "From the Beginning" set off the flickering light that I would follow on course. After a long weekend of fellowship, prayer, worship, and spoken word from renown women of God as Omayra Font, Sonia Luna, Vanessa Gracia Cruz, Maria Arrazola, among others, Yvette and I were consumed with hope and faith that the best was yet to come. We had the opportunity to catch up on the lost time of nineteen years and all that had taken place in our lives only to find out, it was all with purpose and God had a special assignment on our lives. Government and ministry were the two mentioned among the promises of a healing and breakthrough process.

Bishop Ruddy reminded the women at Redoma of the woman at the feet of Jesus during his crucifixion and crying at the tomb, Mary of Magdala. That made me consider the woman caught in adultery who was told to go and sin no more, forgiven, and chosen to follow Jesus. That woman would need to become processed and equipped, considering she was the first woman chosen to go and tell—in other words, preach what her teacher, Jesus, said. Thinking of her, I saw myself, only this time with the proper leadership, guidance, and preparation.

As I received this revelation, I became hopeful and was able to dream again while challenged to switch gears at Southeastern University, from the doctoral program I was into their School of Divinity.

"Mary!" Jesus said. She turned to him and cried out, "Rabboni!" (which is Hebrew for "Teacher"). "Don't cling to me," Jesus said, "for I haven't yet ascended to the Father. But go find my brothers and tell them, 'I am ascending to my Father and your Father, to my God and your God.'" Mary Magdalene found the disciples and told them, "I have seen the Lord!" Then she gave them his message.
John 20:16–20 NLT

My Prayer Journal: June 12, 2019

I have a burning desire to write and tell my story. I have been wanting to share my experiences with others as much as I can. Lately, rather than talking about it, I have wanted to put it into a book and express everything. I went to Redoma 2019, and that began an awakening toward a deeper healing process at the end of the conference.

I left with a great desire for a breakthrough from everything holding me back from pursuing God's purpose for my life wholeheartedly. I want to experience a life-changing breakthrough that I can live to tell about. I know I have many blessings to thank God for, and all I have for Him is my life. I have nothing to give anyone but my testimony, and I desire to be an inspiration and a help to anyone who struggles with their choices to return to Him. I have questions. Before this journal is exposed, I want to know:

Is this right? Why do I want to do this so bad? Who do I want to read it? How will I know when the time is right? Who will help me? Will I be able to do this with the resources that I have? Where do I begin? What do I write? Is this what God wants me to do? I ask God these questions and I trust in Him. In Jesus's name, amen.

If you need wisdom, ask our generous God, and he will give it to you. He will not rebuke you for asking. But when you ask him, be sure that your faith is in God alone. Do not waver, for a person with divided loyalty is as unsettled as a wave of the sea that is blown and tossed by the wind. Such people should not expect to receive anything from the Lord. Their loyalty is divided between God and the world, and they are unstable in everything they do.

James 1:5–8 NLT

CHAPTER TEN

Bound for a Change

*Don't copy the behavior and customs of this world, but let God transform you into a
new person by changing the way you think. Then you will learn to know God's will for
you, which is good and pleasing and perfect.*

Romans 12:2 NLT

Capricious, Wayward, Double-Minded

I was scheduled to begin seminary on Wednesday, June 26, 2019, at SEU. I
felt nervous, and my thoughts took me to past experiences when all the doors were
opening, and my first marriage was in pieces.

At that time, I did not recognize how angry and resentful I was becoming.
I was so hurt by my husband's lack of understanding. I was full of rage every time
I knew he was drawing further away from me when I felt that I needed him closer.
I was becoming more insecure and vulnerable. I was beginning to fear the worst. I
was seeking purpose and driven by an intense desire to grow, to change, and to be
accepted and loved. I wanted to know that I was relevant and important to him.
I believe that was the first time I realized that could not come from marriage to a

135

man.

I recall reading *Be Angry, But Don't Blow It* by Lisa Bevere. In it she says, "Perhaps you have never broken a physical window. But there is a trail of shattered dreams and relationships. The mere fact that you now hold this book means you're searching for the right balance in your life." That was me! It didn't help me want to stay in that situation once I finished my personal reflection. I was too broken by the past and couldn't fathom the idea of a reconciliation.

Jesus knew their thoughts and replied, "Any kingdom divided by civil war is doomed.
A town or family splintered by feuding will fall apart."
Matthew 12:25 NLT

Some things from my past were buried and resurfacing. I began to write what was brought to my memory on June 21, 2019.

On June 21, 2012, seven years ago, I realized I could no longer remain in the same place. I sought support and direction. My first stop was at Titi Carmen's apartment on Seminary Road in Alexandria, Virginia. Then I began to plan how I would depart from his mother's house that week. By the next day, I was discussing several concerns with my aunt. After five moves within the period of two years, and all the friends' sofas I crashed on for the night, Titi Carmen named me "Gypsy."

My mother-in-law sent me a text message, offering me help. She said, *God is not glorified in your misery. Get up and make a decision, move forward and have peace.* I received the affirmation I was seeking to make the decision as a woman.

Recently graduated with my master's degree and with my boss working on a recommendation for my promotion at DeVry University, I was already admitted into a second master's degree program with Mary Baldwin University and registered for a Public Policy class.

By June 22, 2012, I had interviews scheduled with NSU in Fort Lauderdale, an interview with Mary Baldwin University in Staunton, Virginia (where my unfinished, unrenovated house was located), and an interview with Strayer University in Richmond, Virginia. I answered questions with few words, exhausted emotionally and void of clarity.

That same day, my ex-husband and I attended our last counseling session at Mr. Jones's office in Washington, D.C., Mr. Jones asked him, "So what did you get your wife for her graduation?" He said, "Nothing, because it's a process." He had told me, "My name is on that degree and that is all that matters." I told him I was okay with the separation and we could revisit things in six months. I was done and he said he was too. When we exited the building, he went to the left and I went to the right. I went home thinking it would be my last night in his mother's house. She told us she would be leaving for a weekend and hoped we would be okay. I knew it was time to leave.

Can two walk together, unless they agreed.
Amos 3:3 NKJV

My Prayer Journal: June 21, 2019

Today, June 21, 2019, I'm preparing to complete and submit my final paper for the Public Policy course I'm enrolled in. I remember withdrawing from the same course at the master's level in 2012 because I couldn't handle the pressure of another load. I don't know why I ended up on Seminary Road that June, and I don't know why that June I packed up to never return. I don't know why I ended up in the divorce attorney's office, but now in 2019, those memories return.

I'm currently working at a state college financial aid office as a supervisor, enrolled in a Public Policy class, beginning seminary with SEU, and have a job interview lined up at SEU. I just purchased *Be Angry, But Don't Blow It* on my Kindle. Could this be a full-circle moment? This time, I don't want to leave the marriage but am consumed by thoughts of fear, with a house under construction and a child in our life, the Air Force Reserves recruitment process underway, and a church family three hours away from home.

What could possibly be happening? I had gone mad and lost control over my emotions and my ability to filter my own thoughts. All the sudden, I was driving the same 2009 Mini Cooper S down the road in Lakeland, Florida, the place which reminded me of Staunton, Virginia, to gather my thoughts, pray, and ask God for divine intervention. It was as if the movie from 2012 replayed in my face in an instant and I needed to face myself in the mirror.

When everything began to replay, I didn't understand why. I wish I knew. The only thing I identify that I feel all over again is anger. It's as if I have a storage of anger ready to fuel my reactions to Don. Lisa Bevere wrote, "Anger in and of itself is not wrong, but rage and fury escalate it into the dimension of the destructive."

When Don speaks, I become sad. I feel judged, inadequate, unappreciated, and undermined. I feel like an idiot, like he really can't stand me. I feel embarrassed by my own ways, and like everything is wasted effort.

He hasn't demonstrated a gesture of affection, and he is constantly talking about his conversations with his brothers but nothing to do with us in a romantic way. I really feel like this has to happen for a reason, just a reason I don't know. The I struggle with my thoughts. *Is all this my fault? Did I make a mistake? Was I supposed to pursue this relationship with Don?* Suddenly doubts consumed my mind and I was afraid.

I took a drive to the house we were building, then to a McDonalds on the main road near our future home. I was headed nowhere without the light of the Word. I was going to either throw in the towel or move forward in faith that everything would work out regardless of the thoughts the Enemy was trying to place in my head. I went to a hotel in town, let Don know where I was, and he replied, "Take your time."

I was experiencing a full-circle moment that helped me face the truth about my life in the light of the Word. Every time I listened to the Word and went through an experience that brought back memories. It was an opportunity to reckon and repent before the Lord.

In Don's patient and compelling stories of his process as he matured in the Lord, he would talk to me and respect me. He would also say, "You would have really liked the old me." What he meant was that it was the person I would have probably liked ideally, but not the person God had in mind for me and it would take a lot more effort on my part to understand what God is truly equipping us for. I needed to set aside my childish ways altogether and step up to my role as a woman, a mother, and a daughter of the Most High God. I no longer wanted to be a prisoner of my own thoughts.

I remained in the hotel for a few nights while I rested, completed my class assignments, prayed, and self-reflected. Ironically, I was working on an outline for a Public Policy paper on the topic of women in combat roles. I was dealing with a mental battle trying to discover my role as wife, mother, employee, and potential weekend warrior.

I streamed a sermon on YouTube by Paula White-Cain, senior pastor at City of Destiny Church in Apopka, Florida, "A Mama Will Arise." She taught about Deborah, an admirable woman I was intrigued to know more about. Only this time, I was capturing characteristics and traits necessary to lead, influence in Christ as I was preparing my application packet for the Air Force Chaplain Corps.

In Scripture, Deborah, one of the most famous women in the Old Testament, arose, warriors went to battle. Biblical references found in Isaiah 32:9, Judges 4:2, and Judges 5:1–11 depict rebellion and evil which was so evident before a sudden shift would come. The voice of God carried into the government, business, and all of society through Deborah. The Genesis 3:16 prophecy to Eve brought forward great children and multiplication. Women are birthers, designed to carry and give birth to the seed man is designed to produce. It is not a gender issue. It was a sign that resurrection is getting ready to come. Recall the words from God in Genesis 3:15, "You will strike his heel." I felt inspired and empowered to rise up from that past thought pattern and change my attitude. I perceived my husband had been waiting for this moment, but most importantly, God was.

God assigned Deborah to call forward Barak, and under her leadership, deliverance would be brought to the people for sustainment and realignment. Men and women co-create human lives and personify the principals of God. Each comes into the world naked and with a gift. Each gift is given with responsibility. For this purpose, jealousy between man and woman is wrong. In Judges 4, the warriors in Israel were unoccupied or void in action. There was no momentum or movement. God raised Deborah, and when she arose, village life, warrior life, which had ceased, came back. Deborah called forward emotions, feelings, and response, and stimulated the warrior to take action which aligned the plan of God. Men would then be able to govern, guide, and protect.

"Now Deborah, a prophetess, the wife of Lapidoth, was judging Israel at that time. And she would sit under the palm tree of Deborah between Ramah and Bethel in the mountains of Ephraim. And the children of Israel came up to her for judgment. Then she sent and called for Barak the son of Abinoam from Kedesh in Naphtali, and said to him, 'Has not the Lord God of Israel commanded, 'Go and deploy troops at Mount Tabor; take with you ten thousand men of the sons of Naphtali and of the sons of Zebulun; 7 and against you I will deploy Sisera, the commander of Jabin's army, with his chariots and his multitude at the River Kishon; and I will deliver him into your hand'?" And Barak said to her, 'If you will go with me, then I will go; but if you will not go with me, I will not go!" So she said, 'I will surely go with you; nevertheless there will be no glory for you in the journey you are taking, for the Lord will sell Sisera into the hand of a woman." Then Deborah arose and went with Barak to Kedesh."
Judges 4:4-9, NLT

God did this through a woman's prayer life, perseverance, and tenacity. It was time to become the virtuous woman God called me to be. When I confessed to Don that I aspired to become more like the woman in Proverbs 31, he said, "Now you know what I looked for in a woman."

Who can find a virtuous and capable wife? She is more precious than rubies. Her husband can trust her, and she will greatly enrich his life. She brings him good, not harm, all the days of her life.
Proverbs 31:10–31 NLT

During the sermon from Paula White-Cain, I was inspired as she spoke on the historical figures. She described women like Amy McPherson, first media evangelist, and Maria Etter, who in her mid- to late-thirties saw harvest fields and yielded to the call of God after resisting because she was "just a woman." These women did not sit back and take a second-class citizenship. They challenged the unpopular, whether it was gender, ethnicity, or any other discriminations. Righteous women who God used to usher in a season of change include Sarah, Rahab, Esther, Hannah, Abigail, Anna, Priscilla, and Deborah. I denounced all spirits of rebellion, intimidation, and fear in the name of Jesus.

We destroy every proud obstacle that keeps people from knowing God. We capture their rebellious thoughts and teach them to obey Christ.
2 Corinthians 10:5 NLT

Chastened with Love

I always struggled with interrupting Don when he spoke to me, and I repent for that. He would always tell me, "But I tell you the truth, no prophet is accepted in his own hometown." Luke 4:24 NLT. I have also struggled with immeasurable excitement when speaking with anyone about what I'm passionate about. Don would call me argumentative. But I would argue that isn't true. In his patience and concern for me, he was so intentional that one day he did something he'd never done before.

Don would bring me lunch, take me to the nearest park or lake, and just talk. We would spend my lunch hour planning for a better future. We practiced conversation repeatedly. I would listen to him and learn to value everything as if it were the last moment I had left. Something kept stirring up inside of me to want this change for the sake of Christ, and because I understood the blessings in my hands were countless.

Not one day would go by during my six months at Polk State College in which I didn't feel a tug to consider my thoughts, my character, and my perspective on how my relationship with Don could get better. The Lord knew I needed a trustworthy companion more than money, degrees, positions, cars, and beauty. He was teaching me His love.

Love suffers long and is kind; love does not envy; love does not parade itself, is not puffed up; does not behave rudely, does not seek its own, is not provoked, thinks no evil; does not rejoice in iniquity, but rejoices in the truth; bears all things, believes all things, hopes all things, endures all things. Love never fails.

1 Corinthians 13:4–8

Besides writing on a Tupperware bowl lid, "Mami needs to change her mind, think good thoughts," Don reached me in a way no other man had ever done with the truth, love, and the Word of God." One day while I was at work, Don sent me a sermon from Bishop T. D. Jakes titled "The Power of a Changed Mind," inspired by Hebrews 12:6–11. I knew something was changing for the better. I enjoyed the sermon, but the thing I valued most was Don's approach and how God knew how to reach me.

I continued listening to T. D. Jakes, and I recalled listening to him with my cousin Tito in Virginia and with my dad during my time in Alabama. It was then that I remembered my dad and I shared something in common worth reliving: our appreciation for good preaching and good music. I wondered, *Why did I ever stop listening to him?* referring to T. D. Jakes.

I heard that T. D. Jakes, Yesenia Then, and Apostle Guido Raul Avila would be attending *Conferencia Internacional Ministerial* (CIM) 2019 in Miami, and I knew I couldn't miss it. Before arriving, I had purchased and received my copies of *Crushing* by T. D. Jakes and *Renconstruye con los Pedazos (Reconstruct with the Pieces)* by Yesenia Then. At CIM I also purchased three books by Apostle Guido Raul Avila, not knowing what was to come.

If ever there was a time when I needed to change my mind, it was right before the breakthrough I'd yearned to experience since May 2019.

Apostle Guido Raul Avila wrote about the supernatural and aspects such as breaking free from a subsidized and domesticated way of living. He inspired me to reach for a life free from conformity, boredom, and scarcity by accepting the abundance of grace from the Lord. He challenged me to break from the attitude that was molded into a mindset of captivity and oppression to operate the way the world operates. The spiritual tools from his books, *Camino de los Nomadas (Way of the Nomads)* and *Corderos en Piel de Lobos (Lamb in Fur of Wolves)*, taught me to refrain from a life of mixed emotions and spirits that hindered me from living a kingdom mindset.

I would learn about Christ in me, how not to reject or run from the process, and how to preserve my purpose, transformation, and the power of being sent through the true definition of obedience unto God on the road to victory. I wasn't seeing things the same way anymore. Pain was no longer an attraction to me. Sadness due to lacking purpose was becoming a distant thought as I looked forward to leaving pages blank so God could fill them. I could sense something unpredictable, something unexpected and sudden, something as rare as a black swan in the words of Apostle Guido Raul Avila. I believed it would occur because of my growing faith from hearing the Word of God.

I received an entire day's worth of messages at CIM 2019, with each preacher touching on points that resonated with me in my journey from past shame, guilt, insecurities, failures, doubts, and fear, toward breakthrough. I had spent years struggling with a need for approval and control and was believing everything I was told without grasping what God said about me and my identity.

Bishop T. D. Jakes preached a sermon titled "Listen to the Blood," taken from the story of Adam and Eve, Cain, Abel, and Seth. The sermon painted a vivid picture of what I had experienced as a person who felt that nothing had turned out the way that I thought it would, such as in the case of Eve—until God turned it all around for their family, which happened to be history's first dysfunctional family.

Jakes suggested that the Old Testament story of Cain and Abel was a shadow of what occurred in the New Testament with Christ as man in and the Enemy's territory, earth, with a message of hope, faith, and restoration. His message resounded in my spirit, and I knew that what God once promised me was still alive. I knew that retracing steps was not taking steps backwards, though they appeared to be, I was going to be processed before I could move forward because God wanted to prepare me and not it for me, as Yesenia Then concluded with her preaching segment that evening.

I began to recognize the overwhelming pull of the Holy Spirit to let go and let God have His way in my life. I desired more than ever to trust in His plan and not my own. I began to accept that the promises God once spoke over my life were real and that the blood cried out for these promises in my life as the Holy Spirit interceded for me. I knew His thoughts were better than mine, and I trusted Him to lead me to my breakthrough and deliverance.

Therefore, say to the people of Israel: "I am the Lord. I will free you from your oppression and will rescue you from your slavery in Egypt. I will redeem you with a powerful arm and great acts of judgment."
Exodus 6:6 NLT

Encouraged with Love

As I attempted to hold it all together and juggle many roles, I felt the conviction to step back and ask God to reveal a fundamental way for me to manage the various responsibilities. I reserved two Sonia Luna books from Redoma 2019, for devotion and intercession, which would help me navigate the Word of God on topics specific to a woman of virtue, but I still needed deliverance from strongholds that kept me bound for many years.

I reached out to my H.E.C.H.O.S. leader. Absence had made my heart grow fonder for my leader and everything I once had living in South Florida. The purpose and plans God revealed reassured me that despite the distance, He would not forsake me, as I experienced the support and encouragement from leadership at SDV during this time.

Proverbs 27:17 says, "As iron sharpens iron, so a friend sharpens a friend" (NLT). I told my leader that I wasn't sure how I was going to pursue everything without letting go of anything, because I felt like I was supposed to do it all. She asked me questions to probe my thought process. Rather than criticizing me for having goals and dreams, she encouraged and supported me, and reminded me that the Word of God would guide me into becoming a virtuous woman. It was time to have a heart transplant. Not a literal one but a spiritual one.

In my Journal I would write:

Dear God,

I just want you to take control of all my fears, change my heart, help me love the way I am supposed to love, and take me and transform me. If it's true what the prophet told me when I was fourteen, and then when I was pregnant with Danilo at age thirty, "God gave you what you asked Him for; now give Him your talents," what talents was He referring to? I want to know how I can move on with this and trust God. Will he show me the path, the way, and the method to this life? I repent for everything lurking in my heart. I pray for clarity, deliverance from anger, and healing in the name of Jesus, amen.

Create in me a pure heart, O God, and renew a steadfast spirit within me. Do not cast me from your presence or take your Holy Spirit from me. Restore to me the joy of your salvation and grant me a willing spirit, to sustain me. Then I will teach transgressors your ways, so that sinners will turn back to you. Deliver me from the guilt of bloodshed, O God, you who are God my Savior, and my tongue will sing of your righteousness. Open my lips, Lord, and my mouth will declare your praise. You do not delight in sacrifice, or I would bring it; you do not take pleasure in burnt offerings. My sacrifice, O God, is a broken spirit; a broken and contrite heart you, God, will not despise.

Psalm 51:10–19 NIV

CHAPTER ELEVEN

Delivered

On that very day the Lord brought the people of Israel out of the land of Egypt like an army. Exodus 12:15 NLT

My passport to travel outside the United States expired in 2016, but that was not the passport I was given when I received the information for the next step at SDV, an Exodus. This one was going to give me eternal freedom from bondage like never before. Just when I knew that I would want to travel again, dream again, pursue the dreams I thought were long gone, I realized that I still needed to tend to one more detail in my new life with Christ.

I finally felt that I had the relationship I ought to have with Christ, one where I could trust in Him and ask Him anything. I was ready to let go of worries, devote myself completely to Him, and seek Him no matter what I faced. I was learning how to seek Him more in the midst of so many responsibilities and I knew the load would become light. I always carried a load of emotions that burdened my heart and my mind—whether I was accepted or loved by my family and all the influencers who helped shaped me throughout the years.

I wrote down a list of things that shaped me, from my mom, dad, auntie, grandparents, brother, professors, leaders, pastors, ministers, friends, and partners. I thought about the consequences of those influences over my life, the feelings of loneliness, sadness, abandonment, insecurities, bitterness, confusion, bankruptcy, and divorce. I changed my mind about how I would perceive the future.

I acknowledged my negative emotions, my doubtful spirit, my lack of confidence, my need to seek approval of people, and my anxieties. I recognized my intent to control everything in my own strength.

I made a decision. Don always reminded me up to this point, "the Lord said, take on my burdens, for they are lighter." God wanted me to be set free.

I asked God in faith for a breakthrough in my health, in my finances, in my marriage, in my life and in my family, my emotions, and my spirit. I decided to leave behind all anger, bitterness, resentment, pain, and bad thoughts. I wanted to testify. The time had come in which I would be delivered, healed, restored, and saved from my past once and for all.

I will claim you as my own people, and I will be your God. Then you will know that I
am the Lord your God who has freed you from your oppression in Egypt.
Exodus 6:7 NLT

The moment that I decided to accept SDV's invitation to an unforgettable retreat known as "Exodo," I received a pamphlet with a special note from the Pastor that read:

The life of every human being is and will continue to be shaped by events that accumulate over the years and form the character of the person. These events, in addition to other factors such as culture and upbringing, are often not in line with what God wants for you. The Exodus retreat is the event that will begin a process of glorious transformation beginning with your freedom. It is our desire and our duty to help you in the preparation for what will be a retreat. And to this end, we have prepared this passport, as a tool for instruction and guidance. This material that is in your hands is the document that prepares you for the journey where you will emigrate from a life of captivity to the promised land. I exhort you not to stop in front of the obstacles that the enemy wants to raise. Keep going because the best for you is about to come.

After arrival to my exodus, I received the portion of word, forgiveness, and liberty to passionately pursue God's presence. As we began to prepare for the most memorable weekend of my life, I hoped for a life changing experience I could live to share with everyone God put in my path. But first, I had to learn the value of three days. I had to discover the discipline of not wanting to do something out of order, out of emotion, or out of religiousness. I was discovering how to trust, how to release myself into the unknown, into an experience that would transform my mind, my spirit, and my life free from my past of sin and receptive to a future of hope, faith, and love in the Lord Jesus Christ without reservations or wayward thoughts. It was time to surrender all and disconnect completely from everything that distracted me, my work, my family, my flesh desires and listen, follow, and pursue Christ with all my heart and mind connected.

Just as I returned to my cabin at the end of the first night, I was weeping and trying to accept Jesus' sacrifice on the cross yet again. I was convicted. God did this for me, and it was as real in that moment as it had been all my life, not to mention all the times He protected me not letting me die and go to darkness. When I sat in my bed thinking about everything the Holy Spirit was revealing to me as if He was replaying a movie of my life, I noticed a letter on my pillow that read:

Dear Daughter,

I love you. I spilled my blood so you would be clean. In this weekend I will share closely with you. I have chosen this time to tell you how special you are to me. I will open your heart to my words. Let me remove from you all senses of pain and rejection. You are precious in my eyes, and I have created you as you are. Do not condemn yourself by rejecting the forgiveness that I offer you. I want you to start trusting me one step at a time and day by day. Be free. Dwell in my power and in my love for you, and as you do, I will guide you if you allow me.

Acknowledge my presence in everything. I give you patience, love, joy, peace, and life. Search for me, follow me only. May this never fade from your mind this weekend.

Listen to me and I will reveal to you my perfect will for your life. Let my love flow in you and fill you in every way as you touch me. Don't get overwhelmed with your daily needs. You are my responsibility, and I will provide for you in everything. Do not worry about the changes I will make in your life; they will be for your good. Love yourself and everyone around you simply because I love you. Take your eyes off yourself and look at me. I am your provider, the one who changes circumstances when you give me first place. You are my daughter. I believe in you, and I love you unconditionally. Let me give you joy, peace, and love that no one else can offer you.

Your Father and faithful friend,
Jesus

My Prayer Journal: July 19, 2019

Thank you, Lord, because you have answered my request for forgiveness. Thank you, Lord, because they have shown me in Segadores de Vida that there are still servants who honor you and who serve you in spirit and truth. You have shown me your grace and favor by allowing this to happen for me. You have not left me ashamed and you have given me everything I need to fulfill the commitment I have as a daughter, wife, mother, and friend. You have blessed me with your words, with your memory in my heart and with a new opportunity to be in your presence tonight. Thanks for letting me come. Thank you for not leaving me alone. Thank you for giving me a family on earth who has shown me your unconditional love. Thank you for granting me this privilege. Thank you for your love, Father. Thank you for your forgiveness. Thank you for your redemption, thank you for not abandoning me.

Tonight, I accept your forgiveness, your help, your purpose, your guidance, and your instruction, and I give you my trust. I ask you to take care of my family. Let them know where they are that you love them and that everything you do for me you will also do for them. Thank you for my husband, for my family, for my son Danilo, and for everything and everyone around me. Thank you in the name of Jesus. Your Daughter

"And you will know the truth, and the truth will set you free."
John 8:32 NLT

On July 20, 2019, I experienced an encounter with my Father in a cabin house and I finally accepted that not only was I forgiven but that He wanted to use me. "There is therefore now no condemnation to those who are in Christ Jesus, who do not walk according to the flesh, but according to the Spirit" (Romans 8:1). The Holy Spirit visited many of us in the camp and filled us with His loving presence. I was overwhelmed with praise and petition for Him to speak to me and tell me why I was there and what was going to happen. It was liberating to let go of everything and was especially different because I felt things torn out of me from their root for the first time in my life as I screamed repeatedly. I no longer wanted to harbor that which had me bound.

A younger disciple from my group was praying and speaking in tongues without ceasing. The experience was as vivid as that of Acts 2 when we received a visitation from the Holy Spirit. This young disciple wrote on a piece of paper several things God was revealing to her and in one of those utterances she asked me to come sit next to her as she wrote,

Just as God has seen your heart so it will be blessed. If you have faith, says the Lord, do not be overwhelmed. He guards your family and it is with love, not rigor. Holy your hands. You have to pray for someone, and they will be healed. Your friend. Cancer. She will be healed. You lay hands on her and she will be free. Don't be overwhelmed and your blessing will come. Your longing will be fulfilled."

I stored these words in my heart and believed with everything in me that this message came at the perfect time. For me, the reason why God allowed my family to move to Lakeland, Florida, and be farther away from South Florida was clear, and I was going to face a test He was preparing to help me through. I had been dealing with so much confusion on why God had permitted my family to move to Lakeland, but I trusted Him.

It was during my Exodus that these words brought me to my knees. I surrendered everything to the Lord and surrendered my life to His will. I cried out that if it did not come from Him, I did not want it, and that all I wanted to do was serve Him with everything I am. I would no longer try to draw out my own plans and live by my own intellect or desires.

The young lady from my group would pray with me, sing over me, and ask the Lord to protect my ears so that I would hear only Him. I cried and sensed the chains falling off, the weight of anger, sadness, apathy, and despair. I felt my soul letting go of the years of pain and anguish in my heart, and I knew that God was delivering me from these things never to return. I was submerged in His presence on the floor, and the tears were flowing as I basked in His loving presence.

Suddenly I did not feel depression, anguish, rejection, insignificance, low self-esteem, insecurity, or pain from the past. I wanted to pour out my entire being at His feet and just touch Him. I let it go and knew that what Don once told me was true for me for the first time, that I could love my parents, my family, and my enemies the way I knew God loved me. I had worked on my defects for many years. I had exchanged the truth for lies and convinced myself that I could hide it all behind my accomplishments, career goals, and perfectionist ways. But I got up and I told the ladies who were in the cabin, "You can have miracles, you can become a mother, you can be a citizen of the U.S., you can achieve your educational and career goals, you can be married, and you can even build a house, but if you do any of that without God our Father at the center of it all, it is in vain."

I discovered the control I'd practiced and the manipulation of handling my own affairs without the slightest clue that this was separating me from God's perfect plan. The strongholds of witchcraft and generational curses were loosed from me. I was experiencing a breakthrough like never before. The release of these spirits of rage, inconformity, fear, and violence coupled with destructive thought patterns was inevitably going to destroy my family, me, and the purpose God had for my life. I decided to face the truth, myself, acknowledge that it hurt, and forgive everyone all at once. I called them by name, and I declared myself free in the name of Jesus.

The young lady would accompany me to the café, and as we sat at the table to eat lunch, she asked me, "What do you desire?" I continued crying, but I responded, "I desire for my entire family to come back to Him and serve Him." Then when she hugged me and comforted me, the Holy Spirit whispered in my ear, "Why do you keep asking me to forgive you? I have already forgiven you. Just trust me, I will do it. I will fulfill my promise, but you have to trust in me." My heart was overwhelmed with God's love and I was no longer bound by thoughts of abandonment and rejection

My Prayer Journal: July 31, 2019

Lord, I want an opportunity that comes from you. Lord, help me. Use me. Transform me. Direct me. Answer me as you have, Lord. I don't know how to pray. I don't know how to tell you that I no longer want my will. I want yours. I don't want to run or grab what does not belong to me. Lord, take from me everything that does not come from you. Remove every stumbling block. Lord, if it is not in your will, erase it. Lord, I want to see you. I want to hear you. I want to meet you. I want to be your servant, and I want everyone to know you and know of your magnitude and greatness in my life.

Guide me, help me, take me to the place where you and I can communicate, Lord. I want to speak your language. I change my mind and may all my thoughts be for you. Lord, take from me the things you don't like. Mold me into your image. Create in me a clean heart. Wake me up, Lord. Transform my interior and fill me with your anointing. Fill me with your presence. Help me understand more about you. Lord, less of me and more of you. Lord, change my mind. Take away all worry. Lord, do with me what you want not my will but yours.

It doesn't matter if my transformation happens from here in my house or in my workplace. Wherever it is, Lord, it is your will and not mine. Remove all anxiety and carnal desire. Remove from me all lack of understanding. Breathe your presence into me and give me peace and calm in my mind and my heart. I want to listen to you. Lord, break my pride, break my heart. Remove from me any distraction that keeps me from hearing what you want me to hear. Lord, my faith never runs out. You stretch me with power, and with winds from heaven you rejuvenate me. They blow on me, Lord. I beg your hand on me. I beg to hear your voice. I want to be one with you. I want this in the most holy place. I need a meeting with you. Lord, come into my house and fill me.

Bold

In August 2019, about two weeks after returning from my Exodus, I was working at Polk. Brought to my knees in the restroom with excruciating cramps similar to labor contractions I began to cry out to God. I went to my office and let one of my employees know. She suggested that I take a pain medicine and lie in my car for a moment, but I didn't think that was best. I fell to my knees in my office and realized I was being tested.

I texted Don to let him know about the pain I was feeling and the urgency I felt to get up and go pray for my colleague who had been recently diagnosed with cervical cancer. I got up and decided to take one more step in faith. I wanted to be bold in Christ and I did not think twice.

Therefore confess your sins to each other and pray for each other so that you may be healed. The prayer of a righteous person is powerful and effective.
James 5:16 NIV

Not forsaking another moment of opportunity to believe in miracles once again, an onset of labor pains and total dependence on His presence, I drove home for small vase of anointed oil from my nightstand and my Bible and returned to work. I warned my colleague with cancer that I needed to do something God told me to do. I called a Christian witness into my office because as Matthew 18:20 says, "For where two or three are gathered together in My name, I am there in the midst of them." Together we prayed for our colleague. Unbothered by the consequences of this act of faith, I declared I would not leave the job place until the word of God was fulfilled as I believed with all my heart and soul that His sovereign power exceeded my expectations and His promises are yes and amen.

I asked God to heal my friend. I asked Him in Jesus's name to do this and believed because He promised me He would. Not even two weeks later, I received a text message from her and a picture of the doctor's note with negative results, the cancer was gone. My friend was healed from cancer and my faith was taken to a new level.

While one more prayer became an answer, witnessing a healing miracle in someone's life, I was overwhelmed with hunger and thirst for the Word of God. I began seeking signs and wonders, miraculous supernatural things that would keep me aligned with His direction and instruction. The word of God was becoming more evident for me and I was experiencing His presence ever so often. I discovered that I have a heart for intercession and my greatest joy would be in praying for other people's healing and deliverance.

The Lord now chose seventy-two other disciples and sent them ahead in pairs to all the towns and places he planned to visit. These were his instructions to them: "The harvest is great, but the workers are few. So pray to the Lord who is in charge of the harvest; ask him to send more workers into his fields. Now go, and remember that I am sending you out as lambs among wolves. Don't take any money with you, nor a traveler's bag, nor an extra pair of sandals. And don't stop to greet anyone on the road. Whenever you enter someone's home, first say, 'May God's peace be on this house.' If those who live there are peaceful, the blessing will stand; if they are not, the blessing will return to you. Don't move around from home to home. Stay in one place, eating and drinking what they provide. Don't hesitate to accept hospitality, because those who work deserve their pay. If you enter a town and it welcomes you, eat whatever is set before you. Heal the sick, and tell them, 'The Kingdom of God is near you now.' But if a town refuses to welcome you, go out into its streets and say, 'We wipe even the dust of your town from our feet to show that we have abandoned you to your fate. And know this—the Kingdom of God is near!' I assure you, even wicked Sodom will be better off than such a town on judgment day."

Luke 10:10–15 NLT

SECTION FOUR
A Shattered Clay Pot

CHAPTER TWELVE

Where is Boty?

For the message of the cross is foolishness to those who are perishing, but to us who are being saved it is the power of God. For it is written: 'I will destroy the wisdom of the wise,
And bring to nothing the understanding of the prudent. 'Where is the wise?
Where is the scribe? Where is the disputer of this age? Has not God made foolish the wisdom of this world? For since, in the wisdom of God, the world through wisdom did not know God, it pleased God through the foolishness of the message preached to save those who believe."
1 Corinthians 1:18–21

Foolish

Some things do not involve others, only you and God. On August 30, 2019, while many people expected Hurricane Dorian to touch down in Miami, I headed straight to SDV to attend a prayer vigil that Friday evening. That weekend was packed with prayer, reading, and starting my leadership class at the church. Many people said I was foolish for going right into the hurricane's path. But how was I ever going to accept the fulfillment of His promises without sacrifice, without spending time with Him, and without the dedication it would take?

When his parents saw him, they were astonished. His mother said to him, 'Son, why have you treated us like this? Your father and I have been anxiously searching for you." "Why were you searching for me?" he asked. 'Didn't you know I had to be in my Father's house?" But they did not understand what he was saying to them. Then he went down to Nazareth with them and was obedient to them. But his mother treasured all these things in her heart. And Jesus grew in wisdom and stature, and in favor with God and man.

Luke 2:48–51 NIV

My group leader had been praying with me and paused to tell me that she saw me as *Arrebatadora*, English translation "snatcher," which is common in CrossFit training. The objective of the snatch is to lift the barbell from the ground to overhead in one continuous motion. There are four main styles of snatch used: squat snatch, split snatch, power snatch, and muscle snatch.

In a spiritual context, often we are reminded in sermons that "from the days of John the Baptist until now, the kingdom of heaven has been subjected to violence, and violent people have been raiding it" (Matthew 11:12). In this case we are not referring to the violence mankind understands in their own intellect but that of the spiritual realm. The Bible says in Ephesians 6:12, "For we do not wrestle against flesh and blood, but against principalities, against powers, against the rulers of the darkness of this age, against spiritual hosts of wickedness in the heavenly places." Therefore, our fight is not physical but spiritual.

Our duty is to use the weapons that God has equipped us with—prayer, fasting, and His Word, which is light in the midst of darkness. This was not the first time I heard that about myself, but I was finally going to embrace who I am. All I could think about was grasping each moment and enjoying my new season. I knew God had beautiful plans for a territory such as Lakeland, Florida, where it had pleased Him to send my family. I could imagine the group of people who would come with me from three hours away, and I could envision how the church would expand as He trusted me to be a vessel at SDV, to be aligned, purpose-driven, and one hundred percent on board with the mission and vision, to reach all of South Florida and impact the world.

I was eager to spread the news of what God had done in my life thus far, and I believed His thoughts were better than any I've ever had. He was revealing so many good things He wanted to do through ministry. I wanted to be in my Father's house learning about His affairs, and I desired for God to fill me with His Holy Spirit, teach me, and prepare me. This time, I was willing to follow His lead without apology. The cost would be worth it.

And everyone who has given up houses or brothers or sisters or father or mother or children or property, for my sake, will receive a hundred times as much in return and will inherit eternal life."
Matthew 19:29 NLT

The hurricane never came to Miami. I was confident, that moment in the hotel by myself while my family had evacuated to Alabama, that I was finally overcoming fear. I was blessed to have spent the time reflecting upon reading *"El Regreso del Cisne Negro" (The Return of the Black Swan)*, written by Apostle Guido Raul Avila. The main points of this book would have greater impact in my life in a later chapter:

- Never say never.
- Every divine appointment and every miracle have as their stage the physical world in which we live.
- More mystical, less rational.
- You must live in the expectation of faith.
- Open yourself up to the improbable.
- God has a black swan for you because he loves you.

I could only expect the best because the chain of events was yielding fruits like never before. The following steps helped my faith:

- Guard your purpose.
- Keep the honor. Do not stop doing good. If you don't have faith, at least move.
- Keep the heart uncontaminated. Be humble.
- Believe that what God said he will fulfill, he will fulfill. Say, "This will be the day of my miracle!"
- Be malleable and flexible with character for the harvest.
- Be patient.

"If my people who are called by My name will humble themselves, and pray and seek My face, and turn from their wicked ways, then I will hear from heaven, and will forgive their sin and heal their land."
2 Chronicles 7:14

My Prayer Journal: September 11, 2019

Lord, you know my thoughts and my heart. I long for you to do something in my life that only you can glory in. I ask that you do a miracle in my life that surprises everyone, like you have never done in my life. I don't want to sound selfish, and I don't want to envy anyone. I don't want to suffer for anyone else, Lord. It just hurts that everyone around me no longer talks about how good you are and that you have been more than good.

I believe in your miracles, and I believe in your goodness, your love, and your mercy. I don't want to talk about past things anymore. I just want to see what you have reserved for this moment, and I confidently wait for what you will do on my way. Each seed of faith, each step of faith, each decision, each thought, each moment, each move, each sacrificial offering, I dedicate to you. You have been good. I just want to give you back what belongs to you. I want to serve you and I want to have a closer relationship with you. I don't want to hear what they say about you; I want you to talk to me. I want to hear you. I want to see you. I want a special meeting with you. I want to have everything you want for me. I want to dedicate my life to you every day of my journey.

I want to surrender to you. I want to sit at the table with you. I want to know your mysteries. I want more from you. I want anointing to drive away evil spirits so they never return. I want anointing to heal the sick. I want you to use me. I want a word for everyone who needs it. I ask that you take me and use me, Lord. Do not forsake me, because your Word tells me that you will cover me and anoint me, you will guard me from all evil and satiate me with your presence. I ask you, Lord, for your hand on me and for a supernatural healing. I ask for purpose, design, destiny, instruction, demand, allocation, and resources to fulfill my calling in you, for you, and with you. In the name of Jesus, amen.

Very truly I tell you, unless a kernel of wheat falls to the ground and dies, it remains only a single seed. But if it dies, it produces many seeds.
Zechariah 4:6 NIV

With the closing of our new home in Lakeland, my husband's dream car purchase made a reality, and everything aligned for my next endeavor—the military—what could happen next? I was anticipating the moment God would send His confirmation that it was time to move forward. I felt confirmation the moment I knew either I would move, or something would occur that could break me one more time. Only this time it was not a sudden divorce, bankruptcy, or unemployment. It was my fear to work hard for something and burn out. I prayed, I asked God to open the doors. I had hoped to move to SEU for work swiftly. I expressed my intentions to the Office of Student Financial Services at SEU and my prospective director was in full agreement.

I would be cruising through the School of Divinity, seeking for the development I always yearned for, and the full support of an institution aligned with my beliefs and ethical values. It was bittersweet all over again saying farewell to the team at Polk, but they had a reference for any potential opportunity they would encounter. I was confident that they had developed into a fully operational team with a good work ethic, and skills that would transform the environment in which we came to share for six months.

Suddenly, at the six-month mark of being at the college, after experiencing another peak season of serving students and staff in the world of student services, I continued feeling a sense of urgency to disrupt myself from becoming complacent and waiting for the ideal moment to leave. I was being challenged to work harder in what I thought would be a slower pace atmosphere and I was overwhelmed with my desire to pursue the physical transformation that would prepare me for the Air Force Reserves. I was struggling to reach a happy medium between work, life, and the pursuit of my dreams while devoting all my energy and time to my classes at SEU and SDV on the weekends. I asked God for a sign. I sought His approval. I noticed that each time I looked at my watch it was 3:33. I even set my alarm to get up and pray at that time because it was constant after picking up Sonia Luna's book about intercession from Redoma. I knew it was time to pray and seek His direction.

I took a bold step in faith. I took a risk. I resigned from my position, letting Don know we would either close on the house or not, but I was out of there. I always wanted to return to South Florida if God willed it, but in that moment, I was certain I did not want to remain in my particular position at Polk State College. Don and I agreed that the purchase of our house was solely up to me but that there was agreement and support for whatever decision I made at the time in lieu of everything else in the forefront, US Air Force Reserves, school, and continuing forward with a potential opportunity at Southeastern University. When I walked out of the human resources office at Polk, it was 3:33 p.m.

It was a decisive moment. Around the corner from a global convocation to a twenty-one-day prayer and fasting from Yesenia Then ministries. As soon as I left the HR office at Polk after giving my two-week notice on October 1, 2019, my phone rang, I was called for an interview at Polk for another registrar opportunity. It was too late. I was convinced that it was not about another promotion. I needed to move in full faith that I was on the correct path, letting go. On the evening of my last day at Polk, I received the approval to move forward with the appointment at the MEPS in Miami within two weeks.

"Call to Me, and I will answer you, and show you great and mighty things, which you
do not know."
Jeremiah 33:3

My Prayer Journal: October 10, 2019

Today was my last day at Polk State College. I opened the Bible I received as a graduation gift from Montclair Tabernacle Church of God in 2008. Inside I found the United States Air Force Officer Programs business card my Air Force retired friend had given me in 2009 when I talked to her about the Marine Corps. I also found a written list of things God could expect from me in 2014 when I moved to Florida: "to seek God more, read my Bible more, pray, fast, and serve."

Today I believe I was reminded of why I have never been conformed and what God has brought back to my life for such a time as this. I want to take a moment on my day one of this twenty-one-day fasting challenge to dedicate my dreams and desires to God, present my life before Him, and ask Him to lead me and take me through the process and transform me according to His will. I want to ask God to be with me, to guide me, to help me, and to lead me with revelation, direction, and instruction, in His perfect plan. I believe I am here today because, regardless of the circumstances and scenarios I have lived through since 2008, today marks the definition of a second chance. A new opportunity for restoration.

I praise God, I honor God, I am one hundred percent devoted to God. My heart, mind, soul, and entire life belong to Christ, my Savior and redeemer. I trust in you, God, and have faith that every step is ordered by you, and that your love and faithfulness will never fail me. In you I trust. In Jesus's name, amen.

No one will be able to stand against you all the days of your life. As I was with Moses,
so I will be with you; I will never leave you nor forsake you.
Joshua 1:5 NIV

CHAPTER THIRTEEN

Predestined

I knew you before I formed you in your mother's womb. Before you were born I set you apart and appointed you as my prophet to the nations.
Jeremiah 1:5 NLT

It was Saturday again. "The day after this, the day before that." I woke up with a ticket to *Mujeres de Influencia* and slightly discouraged. I had reserved my spot to attend this conference since the summer. Last year I had been online from home in West Palm Beach. It was a year later. My promise, the miracle I was believing for, was suddenly interrupted. I had invited over twenty women to go with me. No one accepted. I began listening to Nimsy Lopez, a Christian singer, on Facebook Live as she worshiped. Moments before she called on her husband for his segment of preaching, I thought, *What am I doing? I'm supposed to be there right now.* I went to the garage and told Don, "I'll be back. I am going to snatch my miracle!"

Then she called to her husband, and said, "Please send me one of the young men and one of the donkeys, that I may run to the man of God and come back.

163

So he said, "Why are you going to him today? It is neither the New Moon nor the Sabbath.
And she said, "It is well." Then she saddled a donkey, and said to her servant, "Drive, and go forward; do not slacken the pace for me unless I tell you." And so she departed, and went to the man of God at Mount Carmel."
2 Kings 4:22-25

On that day, October 20, 2019, as I approached the RP Funding Center in Lakeland, Florida, I remembered one year before when I heard the word of the Shunammite women from 2 Kings. I was going to the same event to hear a word from God once again. The day before, I had learned that I had a mass in my right breast and wouldn't be able to move forward with my Air Force application unless an ultrasound proved it was benign.

Before heading out that morning, I asked my husband to touch the mass and he felt it there, almost the size of a golf ball, as I described how everything played out at the MEPS in Miami. I told him I was optimistic. I remembered what the Lord did for my friend at Polk, and I knew miracles were real. I was convinced a test of faith was necessary a few months before and I believed my faith was so big that the mass would disappear.

When I arrived at *Mujeres de Influencia*, Nimsy was singing "Proceso," a song I had been listening to for seven years. I felt the knot in my throat and burst into tears. As I walked in, the worship intensified, and my arms went up high as my spirit was ready to receive the good news. I texted my husband, *This mass is going to disappear in the name of Jesus!*

Soon after that, Nimsy's husband, Micky, began ministering and told us to raise our hands and declare the word of healing over our life, our family, and our community. My body trembled in the presence of the Holy Spirit, and I was overwhelmed with His touch. With trembling hands and legs, I placed my hand on my breast and didn't feel the mass. Praise God, it had disappeared.

During intermission, I went to the tables with ushers to testify, desiring to get the word to Nimsy and Micky of what had just happened. I also wanted Pastor Roberto

Orellana and his wife to know, so I wrote them a letter.

The usher told me, "Listen, you know what just happened? God healed you. Now when you go to the doctor, no matter what they tell you, believe. Don't worry about the process you may have to go through. Hold onto the word of healing and believe it is done." I said, "Amen." I believed a miracle had happened, and I was prepared to move forward with the process.

On the morning of November 5, 2019, I stepped onto the SEU campus and sought a quiet place to do some research for the Old Testament course I was enrolled in. I passed by the Bush Chapel on campus and heard worship, only to realize Tuesday morning chapel service was taking place. I decided to pop in and experience a weekly service with the students on campus. Little did I know that place would be transformed by the early portion of the afternoon into a conference hall for the Women's Leadership Conference sponsored by the Center for Women's Leadership (CWL) at SEU. After I finished doing some research at the campus library, I stopped by the conference and was invited to sit and listen. I would be seated at the table with my soon to be director. That's right, because during my time of prayer and fasting, I had received the phone call from the Director of Student Financial Services at SEU with an offer to work at the main campus.

I was counting down the days to start work at SEU, but I still needed to take care of some loose ends with my USAF recruitment process for the Reserves. I had explained the steps I would need to take and I was counting on support from beforehand. It was as if everything was lining up in my favor and nothing would change my mind about it. I remember praying in that moment of reflection after listening to Dr. Ingle's segment about perseverance. I had to leave shortly after because I was on my way to West Palm Beach to my group leader's house, not forsaking an opportunity to be in person at group. I'd be staying the night at my brothers before a 0500 appointment at MEPS in Miami the next morning. I could not see the obstacles, I could only see the hand of God protecting the details, the places, the people, and the plans.

My Prayer Journal: November 5, 2019

Lord, thank you for today. Thanks for everything you are doing. Your fulfillment is perfect. Thank you, Lord, for your love, your goodness, for your provision. Thank you, Lord, because you have always been there with me. Lord, I ask that what comes my way prepare me to be better in you, with you, and for you. Lord, I praise you and honor you with my life. I ask that you always guide me and allow me to live a life completely dedicated to you. Lord, I ask that you strengthen me and that you give me wisdom. Lord, I ask that you fill me with your love for others.

Make me listen and make me understand your way. Lord, mold me, prepare me, and use me for your glory. Don't let anything happen to me other than your will. Thanks for your coverage. I trust you. I praise you, exalt you and honor you. Thank you, Father, for being my Father. In the name of Jesus, amen.

Fearfully and Wonderfully Made

On November 6, 2019 after my second appointment at MEPS in Miami, I drove back to my home in Lakeland. I was cleared for the next step at MEPS since I had made weight! After weeks of fasting, praying, walking, and expectancy, I reached a goal I was unable to reach in 2009, a target weight to become an officer in the United States Air force Reserves. I was one step closer and one more appointment away from complete clearance. I was hopeful and scheduled to return on November 18 to prove that I would be clear from any mass in my breast.

The following day, November 7, I drove north to Jacksonville, Florida, for the Wonder Women Conference sponsored by One Quest International. I was excited to participate in some of the more fun activities, like prophetic painting and dancing workshops. On the two evenings I spent at the conference, various topics were discussed, such as "The Father's Heart for You," "Armed & Dangerous Now," "Live in the Spirit, Rule in the Future," "Mentoring Generations," and "Fun as a Necessity, Not an Option." While these topics helped me remain focused and aligned to what I was purposefully seeking, I realized a pain in my underarm that was persisting.

Again, during this event, I prayed and experienced a relief during adoration. I experienced not only a degree of faith that I had never experienced before hearing Kat Kerr, author and revelator, as she talked about revelation she has received from heaven, but also a new perspective on my willingness to seek complete deliverance and supernatural gifts from God. I knew I was made with purpose, I was called on purpose, and I was chosen for a purpose.

> *I praise you because I am fearfully and wonderfully made;*
> *your works are wonderful, I know that full well.*
> *Psalms 139:14 NIV*

It would take more than this book to reveal and discuss the marvels that I have heard from different platforms teaching about the supernatural and the things to come. But in the brief time frame since my experience at my Exodus with my church, I began to receive new invitations and enlightening revelation that changed my outlook on what to expect—nothing less than good from God. I take a moment to inspire you to seek further than what you have already known. Otherwise, it is not worth recounting and recollecting the past experiences and asking God for more. Being renewed is a process and discovering His mysteries is a mystery in and of itself. But through intercession, adoration, and divine revelation, we come to understand the meaning of life and what we look forward to as His kingdom come and His will be done on earth as it is in heaven.

Rather than dwelling on what was not understood in the past, looking into divine healing became my utmost desire, crossing into realms of faith I had never discovered before. I became hopeful in everything that is good. I even gave more concern to things as they pertained to the upcoming elections, the governing agencies, and the angelic activity. Not only had passages taught me more about women in the Bible, I also discovered a new sense of worth for my life.

Therefore, since we have been justified by faith, we have peace with God through our Lord Jesus Christ. Through him we have also obtained access by faith into this grace in

which we stand, and we rejoice in hope of the glory of God.
Romans 5:1–2 ESV

One of the most memorable moments at the event were the key notes that I wrote and kept in my mind as I proceeded through the next steps for 2019. Kimberly Kerr Collins, Kat's daughter, spoke on the first night and I remember these words: "He calls us back to come with our testimony. When they call you, come with your testimony." By faith I knew my value, my worth, and that His renewal was on the way. I no longer estimated what I was worth.

I no longer doubted His capability or what I was here to do. I recognized that I am His, my body is the temple of the Holy One, and He shielded me. I knew I was victorious in Him and His intentions were not the same as what I once believed about myself. I was no longer what Mom, Dad, magazines, books, social media, or anyone else said about me. I was made with love and I was to love because He loved me first. I would no longer compare myself to my past, to others, or to a different definition of worth.

I knew that everything was about time. Giving God my fullest intent, time, and prayer was pivotal in walking by faith. I had expectations for many years, yet I knew that it was not about my expectations. It was about His will. I wanted a relationship with God that would push me forward and higher. Kat Kerr talked about her intentionality and how many years she spent devoted to seeking God until one day Jesus came in Spirit and took her to heaven and hell for revelation so that she could speak about what she had seen.

Though my past was loaded with bad moments, losses, and challenging times, I was convinced that God wanted me to look to Him. Like John the revelator, the Holy Spirit will reveal to us what God wants us to know. Many of us have a hard time believing this because it would be too much to bear. Jesus said,

"There is so much more I want to tell you, but you can't bear it now. When the Spirit of truth comes, he will guide you into all truth. He will not speak on his own but will tell you what he has heard. He will tell you about the future. He will bring me glory by

telling you whatever he receives from me. All that belongs to the Father is mine; this is
why I said, 'The Spirit will tell you whatever he receives from me.'"
John 16:12–15 NLT

My bottom line was in asking Him about every detail in my life—what I was to do, where I was to go, how I was to do it, and if I ought to. I wanted Him to be the author and illustrator of every detail in my life. I tell you this now because it would have been impossible to face what was to come if I did not choose the way I did when I reached a crossroad.

When Kat Kerr shed light on some key takeaways that resonated with me, I continued to ask God for more profound understanding of His word. Just as Jesus showed John Himself as the Word, the Word became flesh, John was with the Word. The Word was made flesh and the flesh was the Word," I was beginning to understand that there is much more God will reveal as we earnestly seek Him. I discovered that from listening throughout the sessions that none of God's children were created to live in fear, abuse, or lack. The only one that hates and despises us is the devil. In other words, none of the attacks from the Enemy are from the kingdom of heaven. Therefore, I did not need to accept them. I needed to continue loosing myself from the residual layers of strongholds that once had a grip on my mind and soul. This would be an ongoing journey until I could be healed thoroughly. It was time to bind those things which are to remain within me, grace, abundant life, and a prosperous soul that belongs to Christ.

That is what the Scriptures mean when God told him, 'I have made you the father of
many nations." This happened because Abraham believed in the God who brings the
dead back to life and who creates new things out of nothing.
Romans 4:17 NLT

We always existed with God and we were with Him before time even existed, so getting back to our original design was as important as pursuing His purpose in my life. I learned that I could ask God, "What do you want?" and He might even answer, "What do you think?" He would give me new thoughts as I sought His word and His ways. When I began to know what He thought, I no longer wondered what He thought. I was tired of going from glory to pit, and from faith to no faith. It was time to change my words—what I said about myself—and declare what God says about me.

So all of us who have had that veil removed can see and reflect the glory of the Lord. And the Lord—who is the Spirit—makes us more and more like him as we are changed into his glorious image.
2 Corinthians 3:18 NLT

Baptized

Upon returning from a three-hour trip from Jacksonville, Florida to Lakeland accompanied by my leader on the phone, I calculated about three hours of sleep for another three-hour trip the next morning to Southwest Ranches, for my baptism, only this time, Don would drive down with me and snap video footage. I was looking forward to a second opportunity with a new understanding. Though it was not mandated by my church leaders, when asked by my leader if I desired to be baptized, I considered not doing it. After all, I had been baptized at twelve years of age in Iglesia Hispana Betel. But I wanted a new experience, and I prayed. She did not persist, she just waited for me to change my mind and come to my own conclusion about my next steps. I wanted to experience unity and connection with the body of Christ I longed to be a part of and be an active participant of everything that meant being cleansed.

When a potter is throwing a pot, water is used to keep the pot and the hands wet. This is so the clay can be worked into a cone shape. The concept of "wheel wedging" helps condition the clay while keeping the clay centered on the wheel. According to a step-by-step guide written by Marie for Potterycrafters.com, "wedging may very well be one of the least liked, but the most important parts of the pottery-making process. Whether by hand or machine, it has to be done."

For by one Spirit we were all baptized into one body—whether Jews or Greeks, whether slaves or free—and have all been made to drink into one Spirit.
1 Corinthians 12:13

I began testifying to my family and former pastor about what was beginning to take place in my life. When I shared with my childhood pastor that I had been baptized at SDV, she asked, "Why did you get baptized again?" I thought, *As if God can't give a second opportunity to those who truly desire one.* She has always been a close friend to my mom. I knew that she knew about my past because Mom told me that she was the only person she ever shared my story with. But my mom would tell me that her pastor's advice had been, "Do not share this with anyone else to protect her testimony."

When I realized that my testimony would be a weapon to take down strongholds, heal the sick, and set the captive free, I began to speak. I no longer felt intimidated. I no longer wanted to keep my mouth shut. I no longer felt that it was a testimony I was protecting but the Enemy I was no longer covering for. The tenacity and boldness that I had proven in a former life of sin intensified within me to live for my Father out loud. I was moved to thoroughly break every chain from past religious beliefs, customs, and traditions which brought a spirit of oppression, confusion, and condemnation. I was seeking the Holy Spirit's direction in everything, even as I prepared for wilderness training.

Therefore if anyone cleanses himself from the latter, he will be a vessel for honor, sanctified and useful for the Master, prepared for every good work.
2 Timothy 2:21

My Prayer Journal: November 20, 2019

Dear God,

Thank you for your blessing and for everything you will do from now on. I am in your hands, and I ask that you be the beginning of my days and my only reason to live. I ask you to keep me and help me to be the best daughter, wife, mother, disciple, friend, sister, and servant. May I never step away but persevere in everything. I thank you for the miracle of work and your way of meeting every need. In you I am trusting. Your hands will hold me. Thank you, Father, in the name of Jesus. Amen.

The blessing of the Lord makes a person rich,
and he adds no sorrow with it.
Proverbs 10:22 NLT

It was not long after I began my job at SEU that I received the phone call from the doctor's office in Miami confirming that I needed a biopsy of my right breast. I remained hopeful even while experiencing something that would delay my next steps toward the military once again. I went to tell my director about my situation, and she empathized and shared with me that my other supervisor had recently been treated for breast cancer. She assured me that the team would pray for and support me through the process.

All I could do was smile and pray, telling God I was willing to go through the entire process no matter what in order to fulfill His will and not mine.

And He said, "Abba, Father, all things are possible for You. Take this cup away from
Me; nevertheless, not what I will, but what You will."
Mark 14:36

My Prayer Journal: November 24, 2019

Be careful what you wish for!

Thank you, Lord, for today! I want to appear before you with a heart of regret for the complaints and for the discouragement I have felt during this week. I want to thank you because not only did you give me work this week, but you provided more. Even in time you granted me grace and you extended my days and my energy to fulfill each responsibility. I thank you for always supplying and giving me your favor and your mercy.

Lord, I ask you to continue searching in my heart. Lord, it is not easy to serve and handle all responsibilities. I feel that what I want becomes more impossible while everything I must do for others becomes a priority. I don't know how to do what I must do, but I also don't know if it is really what I'm supposed to be doing. Lord, I want to fulfill my tasks, but I feel that all my time belongs to the process and the sacrifice. I do not know what to do. I feel worried and unprepared to fulfill my assignments because I am more aware of other people's emergencies.

Lord, if I have not been responsible in serving and managing what you have given me, I ask for your forgiveness and mercy. I ask you for wisdom. Lord, I ask you to help me be better in everything you ask of me. Lord, order my steps and do not allow me to go astray. I ask you, Lord, to free me from all burdens, from arguments, from confusion, from weariness in the name of Jesus. I ask you to give me purpose. Thank you for your abundant grace and favor. Cover me, and fill me with your grace and help me in the name of Jesus. Amen.

Yes, everything else is worthless when compared with the infinite value of knowing Christ Jesus my Lord. For his sake I have discarded everything else, counting it all as garbage, so that I could gain Christ."
Philippians 3:8 NLT

Commissioned

The first time I had to prepare a sermon as a seminary student, I had little to no understanding on the methods of preparing a sermon let alone how to preach, the objectives, the purpose, and whether I was equipped for such a task. I was led by the Holy Spirit to choose the passage from Joshua 1:1–9. I share this with you because it became a part of the journey to the greatest conquest that would require courage.

You may have never thought the day would come when God would speak His assignment for your life in such a way as He did with Joshua, but He does. One thing we can be certain of is that He has a greater purpose for each of us, but I also want to encourage you to always remember the purpose is greater than "me" or "I."

God has already commissioned all of us, according to Matthew 28:19, "Go therefore and make disciples of all the nations, baptizing them in the name of the Father and of the Son and of the Holy Spirit." This Scripture represents the truth behind why we are encouraged to listen to God and why, when we're not certain, we should seek His knowledge, wisdom, and understanding. God has promised we can ask, and it will be given unto us.

As I began to follow the steps, I discovered new things about myself. For example, fears I could overcome with faith and deception I could overcome with the truth of the Word of God and only with the help of the Holy Spirit. Joshua 1:1–9 became a training ground for me to pass the test of faith and obedience while attempting to overcome fear, emotional distress, and doubt. I had the promise, but I needed to possess it. Each step in the process of developing a sermon was as tedious as each step applying for the Air Force to get to MEPS. From the research, to obtaining medical records from various medical facilities I had been to over the past ten years, I was digging into a past while looking into the future and training physically to make weight while breaking from defeated thoughts. I was learning how to follow instructions, and it was important to discover how God realigns our purpose when we obey and take courage. I came up with these strategies, which may be helpful to you as well as we go through our journey toward conquest:

- Be attentive to God's commands (Joshua 1:1–9).
- God vs. man (God is always the Hero!) (Joshua 1:5–7).
- Faith and obedience (Joshua 1:8–9).
- God is my hero. He is your hero. He is our hero through His sovereignty, fulfillment, and everlasting promises.

God promised Joshua, like Moses, that He would be with him, not fail him, not forsake him, not leave him, and not abandon him wherever he went. He promised success and prosperity. God is with us wherever we go. God is our instruction, our encouragement, our faith, our guidance, our deliverer from all evil and adversity, our strength, our promise keeper, our leader, and our hero in all that we do. He will command us and we will succeed, we will prosper. Philippians 4:13 says, "I can do all things through Christ who strengthens me."

When you believe this, you will be encouraged, strengthened, secure, and affirmed in the Word of God. When you follow the instruction from His Word, you will feel joy and hope in the midst of crisis and turmoil because you'll know that God is with you and that what God promised, He will fulfill. Not only will the territory be yours, but you will succeed and prosper in all that you do, and no man will be able to stand against you. Say it with me: "I believe it!"

SECTION FIVE
Restored by Grace

CHAPTER FOURTEEN

A Plan for a Hope and a Future

The people will no longer quote this proverb: "The parents have eaten sour grapes,
but their children's mouths pucker at the taste." All people will die for their own sins—
those who eat the sour grapes will be the ones whose mouths will pucker.
Jeremiah 31:29–30 NLT

The Return of the Black Swan

Do you remember the black swan from chapter twelve? In *El Regreso del Cisne Negro (The Return of the Black Swan)*, author Guido Raul Avila writes, "When the pillars of our life wobble, instead of looking for the cause, we tend to hold on to them tighter. From the probability, a black swan is an unusual event and, therefore, unexpected, with positive or devastating effects since you are not prepared to face it and, at best, it was only possible to imagine what would happen to others, but never yourself."

How do you determine if you're witnessing a black swan? Not only did I discover literal black swans during a drive to a lake with Don and Danilo, but I discovered the swans are said to have been brought to Lakeland from England.

179

According to an article written for lakemorton.org:

"Queen Elizabeth, known to be a little tight with a farthing, agreed to send a pair of swans to Lakeland if the city would pay the cost of capture, crating, and shipping, estimated at $300. Eventually the money was raised and a pair of White Mute Swans from England were released on Lake Morton on February 9, 1957. Descendants of that pair continue to grace the city's many lakes; today there are more than 200 birds, including White Mutes, Australian Black Swans, White Coscorba Swans from the Falkland Islands, Black Neck Swans from South America, white pelicans, ducks, geese, and other species.

Lakeland has learned its lesson and is very protective of its swans now. There is an annual swan round-up, at which time the graceful birds are inoculated against disease, and the city provides feeding stations and breeding pens along Lake Morton's perimeter. The swan is now the city's official logo."

In *El Regreso del Cisne Negro (The Return of the Black Swan)*, Avila addresses these supernatural causes. Brace yourself because my takeaway from his book may remind you of some of the events we have witnessed globally in 2020:

- The event is surprising and has not happened before now. Very few, if any, could have thought that it would happen.
- The impact is huge, whether positive or negative.
- Once it happens, the explanation of why it happened and how it could have been foreseen is relatively simple. Everyone becomes adept at explaining it, but they could never foresee it.

Look at the nations and watch—
and be utterly amazed.
For I am going to do something in your days
that you would not believe,
even if you were told.
Habakkuk 1:5 NIV

Reset

In my case, on January 9, 2020, following three appointments at Moffitt Cancer Institute of Research in Tampa, Florida, a new twenty-one-day fasting period with SDV, my usual Tuesday morning intercession with my leaders, and constant prayers from family and friends, I was hoping for a negative result—a glitch on my records and a miracle that everything was just a dream! My black swan arrived.

I took a deep breath when my doctor called me to deliver the news: "You have breast cancer." My mom, my grandmother, and my cousin had recently arrived from Puerto Rico after several earthquakes had shaken the island. I was aware that the process would begin, and it was imperative that I remain calm and plan accordingly with my husband. I thought it was most proper to read the book of Job. It became most comforting, and I surely didn't want to miss out on the guided instruction over people's woes and opinions.

It became my period of "hurry up and wait" as I continued going to Moffit for more scanning, more screening, and consults. I was enrolled in Introduction to New Testament for my MDiv. Right around the same time, Bishop Ruddy Gracia preached "Reset," a sermon about Paul's encounter with Jesus on the road to Damascus based on Acts 9:1–11, and Yesenia Then was wrapping up her series on Revelation on Monday nights, and I was catching up as I ramped up to take a course on Revelation the following term.

It was a divine set-up for a time to study the four Gospels, the accounts of the apostle Paul, the book of The Acts of the Apostles, and Revelation. I was forward thinking with the knowledge SEU was equipping me, coupled with leadership classes at SDV and my own personal journey. My leaders at SDV challenged me to open a Pilot Grupo H.E.C.H.O.S. at my house, and the new disciples arriving from Tampa were well on their way to an Exodus retreat to include my mom coming from Alabama whom I persisted and insisted with. The fast-forward button was pushed when 2020 began.

I had not planned for the "autopsy of a decade" until it was God's perfect way of provoking a reset that would shatter everything "normal," and gear me up for new unimaginable opportunity in places I never dreamed of going: the world of cancer, survival, and recovery. The first step was in trusting Him.

I wrote in my Journal:

I am sitting at my desk at work, finished with my daily tasks. To say I am overwhelmed by God's favor and grace is an understatement. I had been seeking the Lord's guidance for such a long time, desiring to know Him more and speak confidently of His mighty works. I thanked God for blessing me with my family, friends, and ministry the way He did. I was honored to serve Him with my life. I didn't want to ask why. I wanted to know what's next?

I sought to be prepared, and I was still uncertain as to whom I could trust. I wanted to trust people, but I didn't feel like any relationship was strong enough to face this trial and adverse time. I admit, I was afraid of believing anyone, because none of them had shown interest in the details of what we were doing together. I told God, this was between Him and I and I asked Him to make me useful and make me an example for others. All I asked Him was to give me strength during this time. I needed His revelation and guidance.

For as the heavens are higher than the earth,
So are My ways higher than your ways,
And My thoughts than your thoughts.
Isaiah 55:9

On February 6, 2020, I received good news! On Thursday I learned from my doctor the final diagnosis. First, I received a phone call confirming that out of fifty-nine strands of potential genetic diseases, I did not have any positive strands or signs of genetic mutations leading up to cancer. Also, none of the strands stemmed from my mother or my father and they "don't know where it came from." The final verdict on my genetics testing said the cause for my cancer is "unknown." I found a good Facebook meme that day that said, "It ran in the family until it ran into me and God said enough!"

The Holy Spirit led me to a Scripture confirming this truth:

In those days they shall say no more:
"The fathers have eaten sour grapes,
And the children's teeth are set on edge."
Jeremiah 31:29

Hopeful

By February 10, 2020, I was on my way to Moffitt to get a port catheter for my first round of chemo. Four months had gone by since the physician found the mass in my breast at MEPs.

For I know the thoughts that I think toward you, says the Lord, thoughts of peace and
not of evil, to give you a future and a hope.
Jeremiah 29:11

I had been confident in my prayers during these times as I prepared for whatever was coming next. It was my desire to see my prayers of faith turn to reality, but I was only hoping for what I could selfishly hope for—my entire family to come together and reconcile, be restored, and serve the Lord in unison.

I did not want to relinquish anything I had worked so hard for. I was practicing my thoughts and prayers in silence, in my journals, and in the quiet places away from people. The reality was, no one was really focused on the same things as me, I was discovering a new and unfamiliar territory no one in my family had ever traversed, total surrendering without controlling the outcome. It would take unprecedented courage, faith, and hope. It would be a new tough lesson for me.

God saved you by his grace when you believed. And you can't take credit for this; it is a gift from God. Salvation is not a reward for the good things we have done, so none of us can boast about it.

Ephesians 2:8–9 NLT

My Prayer Journal: February 6, 2020

This week has been full of surprises to say the least. After I spoke with my nurse, Dorothy, last Friday afternoon, I became convinced that my process was only beginning. I heard her confirm my diagnosis and affirm my next steps for treatment. On the bright side, my entire family came up on Saturday and we celebrated my little cousin's birthday at the park. On Sunday I went to church and we celebrated *Primicias* (first fruits). By faith I gave my first fruits and received an amazing word from my pastor. I had no idea what to expect every day as the week progressed. I believe the words the pastor declared: "You are free, woman. You are free. You are free, woman. You are free," were for me. I was overwhelmed and excited. I hoped for a new week full of good news.

On Wednesday February 5th, I finally received a phone call from my oncologist. The good news is that my mammogram biopsy showed ER positive, PR positive, and HER2 negative. This is a good thing. The doctor told me I have grade 3 and the cancer is spreading rapidly, but the plan of neoadjuvant chemotherapy is recommended and will reduce the risk of reoccurrence. Immediately after hearing from my doctor, I was relieved. I would be healed and the cancer would not return.

I reached out to share the good news with my family and ministry friends. I was suddenly discouraged when my faith was challenged. Though I did not want to hear people's opinions, some people persisted in sharing their thoughts with me. I was uncertain about sharing any details when it meant I had to hear their feedback. One person told me in a few words what God showed her and challenged me to have "bigger faith," suggesting that I needed to "think bigger." I admit, I was upset. I remember the words from that woman at the conference in October, "Do not believe in the process, just hold onto the miracle that you already received."

Regardless of the steps I needed to endure, I was not concerned with the details as much as everyone else was. Some people told me, "It's dried up," referring to the tumor. Others said, "No man will put a hand on you," or words such as, "Even if it is just one breast needing to be cut off, that is already a victory." Some believed my hair would fall out and advised me to shave my head. But Don would say, "You don't know that. Therefore, don't shave it off. Watch and see." In the long run, no one knew but God. I knew that my faith and hope was not in what I could control or run away from. My faith and hope were anchored in the Word of God and what the Holy Spirit was teaching me each step of the way.

One night, I shared my feelings with my husband. At this point, he was believing and hopeful that everything said was not necessarily true for me. After he shared that with me, I took a drive and prayed to retract all my words and thoughts about people feeling hopeful. I realized I couldn't do this by myself and I needed all the support the Lord was sending to me. I wanted to refuse hearing what they had to say, but I wanted to remain encouraged. By the time I reflected on my feelings, I realized I might not tolerate anyone challenging my faith as I went through my process, but with guidance from the Holy Spirit, I would know in whom I could confide.

Out of the hundreds of livestream services I had listen to, I learned about a scripture that helped me shut down the game of false prophecy in my life once and for all: "If the prophet speaks in the Lord's name but his prediction does not happen or come true, you will know that the Lord did not give that message. That prophet has spoken without my authority and need not be feared" (Deuteronomy 18:22 NLT).

I received peace. In that moment, I knew everything was purposeful. I was at ease and once again shared the good news with my loved ones. Later that Thursday, my doctor called me to inform me that he was officially recommending chemotherapy. He was going to order my appointment for February 10, the following week on Monday to begin with Taxol, and CI DDAC would begin after four rounds of Taxol. Both treatments would extend through summer 2020.

When you go through deep waters,
I will be with you.
When you go through rivers of difficulty,
you will not drown.
When you walk through the fire of oppression,
you will not be burned up;
the flames will not consume you.
Isaiah 43:2 NLT

CHAPTER FIFTEEN

The Waiting Room

I waited patiently for the Lord;
And He inclined to me,
And heard my cry.
He also brought me up out of a horrible pit,
Out of the miry clay,
And set my feet upon a rock,
And established my steps.
He has put a new song in my mouth—
Praise to our God;
Many will see it and fear,
And will trust in the Lord.
Blessed is that man who makes the Lord his trust,
And does not respect the proud, nor such as turn aside to lies.
Many, O Lord my God, are Your wonderful works
Which You have done;
And Your thoughts toward us
Cannot be recounted to You in order;

If I would declare and speak of them,
They are more than can be numbered.
Psalms 40:1–5

On February 11, 2020, I was sitting in bay #4 when Chaplain Sandy Harbour at Moffitt, approached to sit with me during the first moments of my first treatment. After getting to know about me a little bit, she named me

"Martha."
And Jesus answered and said to her, "Martha, Martha, you are worried and troubled about many things."
Luke 10:41 NIV

Chaplain Harbour was gauging my attitude toward everything and helping me understand I was extremely busy with all my affairs. As she spoke to me, I looked to my mom sitting in the chair in front of me. Mom looked at me with sadness, and all I could imagine she might be thinking was, Don't be like me. Chaplain Harbour recommended a wonderful book, *Jesus Calling*, by Sarah Young. This was the same book my eldest and wisest employee from Palm Beach State College, Ms. Sherry, had recommended to me two years prior. Nothing like those full-circle moments!

I took the first round of chemo like a champ. My nurse said, "You did great." That afternoon, I was feeling confident and ready to take on the remaining fourteen rounds with the impression that I could handle the load I had set myself up for.

Little did I imagine, the first round would be the worst I would endure for the duration of chemo, leaving me heartbroken because I couldn't handle full-time work, taking classes, and driving seven hours round trip to church and my pilot virtual women's group all at once. But it was time to become more like Mary, less like Martha. I needed to put down many things and pick up one: constant devotion at Jesus's feet.

It would be a sacrifice that I had to make time for while letting go of so many things I truly had no idea how to manage: classes, leadership, and my waist-length locks of hair. I didn't stop taking classes at my school, and I didn't give up on going to work, but the clock was ticking. It was necessary for me to give it all, for His name to be exalted. It was imperative for me to learn that my activity was not more important than my intimacy with Christ.

The Fourth Cup

Day two after treatment, my Neulasta medicine took effect in my system, causing fatigue, neuropathy, and extreme aching in my legs. I went home early to lay down. My leader sent me a ninety-second clip of Yesenia Then preaching about Jesus Christ in the garden of Gethsemane (Hebrew *gat shemanim*, "oil press") and how some of us may be experiencing a process in which God wishes to produce the best oil, which represents the anointing He deposits in us.

Through the process of crushing, it takes total dependence on Him to realize what God wants to produce in us, from our thoughts, to our decisions, to our character. In Yesenia Then's video clip, Yesenia grabs her glass of water and challenges the listeners to drink the cup with joy because if He gave us the fourth cup, He most definitely prepared us for what is in it to drink and He would produce something out of it that He would reveal.

In the fourth cup Jesus was about to drink, (not a literal cup but a spiritual one), the cup was full of our iniquities, our transgressions, our infirmities, and everything that represented sin in this world. You may wonder, *If He drank it, why should anyone else have to*? Jesus Christ did not have to, but He did. He showed humility and obedience and left us with the power to choose our lot the same way He did. In this moment, He represented the Son of Man, and as God's children, wouldn't we be willing to do the same if it represents glorifying our Father who also raised Christ from the dead? This is the power of love that God showed us in John 3:16, "For God so loved the world, that He gave His only begotten son, that whosoever believe in him, shall not perish but have everlasting life" (KJV).

Believing in Christ may cost us everything we have ever known—our perfectly imperfect conditions, our career, our family, our goals, our dreams—but what good is it to be able to do it all without knowing the love of our Father? I may not be able to convince you with words what my Father showed me through this first cycle of chemotherapy, but I can assure you that trusting God means uncontrollable measures, total surrendering, and sacrifice of self. He wishes to reveal to your Spirit many things about what He says about you. It will take faith, which will inevitably produce patience.

My brethren, count it all joy when you fall into various trials, knowing that the testing of your faith produces patience. But let patience have its perfect work, that you may be perfect and complete, lacking nothing.
James 1:2–4

I wanted my own experience; I wanted to know Jesus better. For all have sinned and fall short of the glory of God (Romans 3:23). Therefore, when it comes to these processes, they are not a punishment to that individual; it is a process and only the one going through the process will know through God's revelation its true purpose. Don't ever believe someone that says, "You are so good, and you don't deserve to go through this." There is truth and hope in the Word of God, and the devil is a liar. Allow God to reveal this to you through His living Word.

The righteous person faces many troubles,
but the Lord comes to the rescue each time.
Psalms 34:19 NLT

Affliction is used for qualification. I know that may be hard to comprehend when we are used to having faith and seeing things as done because we have believed they will happen. We are so set in our ways once we have decided to follow Christ and believe in the impossible. The worse thing we can do is base our process on what God has done in someone else's life. David the psalmist said, "It is good for me that I have been afflicted, that I may learn Your statutes" (Psalm 119:71 AMPC). It is necessary to understand that a process is useful for pruning and equipping us to a good work at various capacities in the name of our Lord Jesus Christ. The form in which we are processed determines the outcome and form God will use us in. As far as I could recall when I received my diagnosis, I knew that He had a plan and it was not vain imagination, it was my reality and my new constant—faith and obedience.

Even Jesus said, "Father, if you are willing, take this cup from me; yet not my will, but yours be done" (Luke 22:42 NIV). But He took the cup, he drank it, and demonstrated his obedience unto God our Father. By faith, we know that He has overcome this world and all God asks of us is to trust in Him just like Jesus Christ did.

The week of my first round of chemotherapy was the first time in my life I realized how many nerves I really had throughout my body, when neuropathy kicked into overdrive. I cried, overjoyed, and suddenly I knew I had been chosen for this so that I could testify of His works. I can tell you, God is good!

Being confident of this, that he who began a good work in you will carry it on to
completion until the day of Christ Jesus.
Philippians 1:6 NIV

When Jesus Arrived

The third day after chemo treatment number one, I didn't want many people around me. I wanted to take the steps God had for me in faith and trust without the chatter and noise that was ever increasing. Don made my breakfast, kept busy throughout the day, and checked in with me periodically. My mom made me lunch, cleaned my entire house, and came to my bedside a few times.

On one of those occasions, I played Yesenia Then's preaching titled *"Cuando Llega Jesus"* (When Jesus Arrives), and I praised Him prostrate in my bed on that day. My mom made a comment to me, "I know how you feel because I have lived with this pain all of these years," alluding to her chronic fatigue and fibromyalgia. I didn't say anything. But I was determined I would be cocooned in my process and prepared for a metamorphosis, trusting in God alone for every detail of the process. The best part about the fourth cup was that it was the first and the last I would have to take in Jesus's name.

A Good Friday

That Friday evening, Valentine's Day, Jesus showed up, and He served me a cup and bread and we had a feast. Titi Carmen called me and asked me if her pastors in Virginia could pray with me and if I had some grape juice. I never purchase grape juice, but on this occasion, I had some fresh Publix French bread, and some Welch's grape juice Mom had purchased. This would not be a complete celebration if I do not share what the Lord did for my family on this evening as we did communion on Skype and prayed together.

You see, on many occasions growing up in the church, I took communion. I associated this with my understanding of a symbolic reference but limited by convictions which took years for me to receive through revelation. On this occasion, I knew Jesus arrived and set something up for me like never before so that I tell you, he has always heard you also.

And when He had given thanks, He broke it and said, "Take, eat; this is My body which is broken for you; do this in remembrance of Me." In the same manner He also took the cup after supper, saying, "This cup is the new covenant in My blood. This do, as often as you drink it, in remembrance of Me."
1 Corinthians 11:24–25

My Prayer Journal: February 14, 2020

Dear God,

I have been in my bed all day long. The pain I've felt has been intense, and I'm so grateful to have some relief at this time. My mom and husband were champs in helping me, and words are not enough to describe the gratitude I have for them. My bosses wished me to feel better and get well. I was encouraged by many friends and family members to stay strong, and prayers were lifted.

Lord, with all the gratitude that I have, I rest with peace that you have me in the palm of your hands and that I will be okay for the duration of this journey. I am forever grateful for the support and help for sustaining my family and helping me remain calm in the midst of pain. Thank you for showing me your love and compassion and for writing my story for others to know more about you.

Lord, I ask you to cover my family, my job, my school, my ministry, and all my affairs with grace and favor, and that you lead me on your path as I journey along with this treatment. Lord, I feel the pain, and I don't know how I will feel every day, but I ask for strength from you and abundant grace every day. In Jesus name, amen.

A Message from Abba, Lord Yeshua, and the Spirit to Joanette

Daughter rejoice, rejoice daughter, because the worst is over. You went through yours, for your family. I, your God, chose you, I your God, because I bring unity to your house. I have people praying, interceding for you. Nothing will happen that I will not allow, because you are mine. Since you were born, you have been mine. Mine, only mine, and nobody takes away what is mine.

But I bring unity to your house, I bring unity to your family, to yours. And many will see this and believe through you because I lift you up—strong, victorious, and powerful. What, do you not know that I am raising Deborahs and Esthers in these times?

Sing, and your praise will rise to me. And it will be medicine for you, it will be medicine for you. My Word will be medicine for you, it will be medicine for you, because I am there with you. And I have not left you, I will not leave you.

And right now, angels surround you. I fill your house with angels. Outside, inside, wherever you move I am going to be. And do not worry about your child, because I watch over him. Angels surround him, watch over him, care for him, care for your husband. Your house is in my hands. Trust, daughter, trust. I, Jehovah, I am your God, I am your Father, I am your Lord.

Your prayers have risen to me, and I have heard them and have come to you because you have been dear to me. And I will return to you, and I will visit you and I will be with you from the beginning to the end, and you will know that I, Jehovah, am your God who has not left you nor forsaken you.

And your Father, who has seen in secret, will reward you in public. Because I planned everything tonight for you. This is not my hour; this was for you, for you. Because it is not my hour, it was your hour; it's your time. Enjoy yourself and rest. Cry out to me. I will always be with you, I will always be there. This is your hour. And this was not only my dinner, but yours and mine. You were my guest, daughter.

On February 15, 2020, I was blessed to have time for rest and family. Mom took me to the nail salon. Ms. Tina was so kind. She shared her husband's story of cancer and was very thoughtful and patient with me. Later, my dad arrived. It was a day of rest. Praise God, my SDV leader called me just after I had prayed about my leadership classes at the church and what the best course of action should be. She told me to not worry about classes for now. I realized that I needed to be obedient and rest during this process. My leader said, "Perhaps you will not be able to host your Pilot Group H.E.C.H.O.S. from home with the same intensity, but we will take things one day at a time" or until I had fully recovered. I secretly hoped for a virtual group. God's everlasting love was shown through my ministry's love and compassion in the midst of this process that I was going through.

During my parents stay, we watched a few sermons from Yesenia Then in Venezuela and Ruddy Gracia's "Reset" and "Marked by Fire." We listened to worship music from Egleyda and Rene Gonzalez. I thanked God. He was granting me with rest, peace, and a good word despite the chemo process. I was able to rest a few hours.

The Message Bible tells us in Philippians 4:6, "Don't fret or worry. Instead of worrying, pray. Let petitions and praises shape your worries into prayers, letting God know your concerns. Before you know it, a sense of God's wholeness, everything coming together for good, will come and settle you down. It's wonderful what happens when Christ displaces worry at the center of your life."

But as for me, I watch in hope for the Lord,
I wait for God my Savior;
my God will hear me.
Micah 7:7 NIV

Unstoppable

In my moments of prayer, all I could think of was how great God is. I would listen to sermons, study His Word, and receive the peace in times of uncertainty. As the pandemic intensified, so did the prayers and Scriptures that anchored my soul. When I heard my family, my friends, and my coworkers speak, I would meditate and consider my thoughts. I was certain that no one else knew my thoughts or concerns better than God. I wanted to be in all the places I was familiar with—at church, in class, and outdoors—but I was beginning to experience the side effects. The week after my first treatment, one colleague asked me, "How was church?" I was mocked because of my seven-hour journeys every Sunday to Southwest Ranches. I would hear voices from anyone I gave ear to, "You will need as much rest," "You aren't driving down there are you?" I would smile.

Like Naomi in Ruth but like Elisha in 2 Kings 2:19–25, my interior was burning with desire to be in Bethel (in Hebrew, "the house of bread"), with the people of God. "Then she arose with her daughters-in-law that she might return from the country of Moab, for she had heard in the country of Moab that the Lord had visited His people by giving them bread" Ruth, 1:6). Perhaps they may have meant well. I knew that I wanted to grab a hold of the mantle of anointing that could take down strongholds of apathy, barrenness, fear, and all the sickness from the souls of those who desired to see God's glory manifested in Jesus' name. Praise God SDV would be one of the few churches to never close during COVID-19 and we would see these miracles manifested in the greatest season of harvest to come.

Then the men of the city said to Elisha, 'Please notice, the situation of this city is pleasant, as my lord sees; but the water is bad, and the ground barren." And he said, 'Bring me a new bowl, and put salt in it." So they brought it to him. Then he went out to the source of the water, and cast in the salt there, and said, 'Thus says the Lord: 'I have healed this water; from it there shall be no more death or barrenness.' "So the water remains healed to this day, according to the word of Elisha which he spoke. Then he went up from there to Bethel; and as he was going up the road, some

youths came from the city and mocked him, and said to him, 'Go up, you baldhead!
Go up, you baldhead!" So he turned around and looked at them, and pronounced a
curse on them in the name of the Lord. And two female bears came out of the woods
and mauled forty-two of the youths. Then he went from
there to Mount Carmel, and from there he returned to Samaria.

2 Kings 2:19–25

A Quarantine Birthday

Dear Thirty-three,

This has been the BEST year of my life. From the moment I was anticipating meeting you, I was joyful and ready to learn. I want to say thank you for the time we have spent together. We have only been with each other for one year and it feels like an entire lifetime. I still remember when you told me, "Hey, did you know Christ was thirty-three when he shed his blood for all of humanity?" You also told me, "He only spent three years doing ministry, miracles, and teaching his disciples before it was his time to fulfill what he came to do on earth." I was so inspired by you to aim high and get on track for the wonderful things God promised me as a little girl.

Shortly after meeting you, you came along the journey with my family to Lakeland, Florida, and kept us excited for the new home we built upon the rock. We knew this one was good. We had peace, because you told me agreement had to be priority and it was going to be the biggest decision I would be making in the midst of uncertainty. You were so understanding and helpful every time I needed to explain myself, because you would suggest new ways in communicating.
You reminded me to trust in the Lord with all my heart and to never lean unto my own understanding. You kept me focused and acknowledging God in all my ways. In fact, you made sure that I went to every prayer meeting, church service, lesson, and group meeting to gather myself and fellowship with many other women of like-mindedness. You helped me make new friends and trust them with very personal areas of my life that needed immediate attention.

You asked me if being a virtuous woman was even a thought and held me accountable every time I wanted to throw a fit. I laugh now because I know it was funny watching me, but the reality is, you were a godsend to awaken me into a growing stage that He knew would happen in LOVE. You didn't give up on me when I started sharing more of my deeper thoughts and realized I had bigger issues I wanted to overcome. You talked me through it, and when I was quiet, you helped me think more. You told me to be slow to speak when I was angry and to be persistent in love and faith. You showed me how to give everything for nothing.

You taught me how to dare and believe in what I had never seen so that I could see what God would do. By the time we drove toward a hurricane together and saw it bypass us, we celebrated our growing faith with bigger hope. I say this because the HOPE I needed was still unknown.

I still remember when you helped me with my graduate classes, and one in particular that took us for a spin was Intro to the Old Testament and Hebrew. Who would have known that preparing a sermon would mean trial by fire! In those days we prepared to preach on Joshua 1:1–9. Do you remember? God said, Do not be afraid or discouraged. For the Lord your God is with you wherever you go.'" It took COURAGE!

We went on so many trips to and from, and you would tell me, "Listen to Him, He is speaking. Seek Him. He wants you to know Him. Look up, look around. He is everywhere. He is taking us, and we don't have to worry about anything." Somehow you eased my anxieties and worries. You challenged me to look passed the obstacles and lean on Christ for the path. My desire to seek, learn, and serve grew into a passion I thought had died. We even met some inspirational people who traced a way and learned so much from them. Once we reached a point of inexplicable motivation, we launched ourselves by faith and you saw me get my hopes up! I strove for those dreams that began at a young age, and you helped me push at max potential and you made sure that I wrote down all the details because they would matter.

Here I am telling you thank you. Thank you, 33, for not giving up on me. Thank you for going with me all the way. Thank you for holding my hand when they said, "You have breast cancer." Thank you for encouraging me with the very words

God spoke to us when we were so busy. Thank you for reminding me every day to get up, try, and move forward. Thank you for the ridiculous faith you showed me.

Thank you for showing me fearless courage and reverent fear for the Lord. Thank you for keeping me on track. Thank you for keeping a record of everything so that I couldn't forget, with my "chemo-brain"!

I believe this journey was so short but worth EVERY DAY and I can't wait till you meet thirty-four. She is going to SOAR. She is going to give back. She is going to replenish. And her NEW LIFE is going to thank you eternally for going through the entire process so that her BEST may be eternal in CHRIST

CHAPTER SIXTEEN

Her Story

The Lord gave another message to Jeremiah. He said, "Go down to the potter's shop, and I will speak to you there." So I did as he told me and found the potter working at his wheel. But the jar he was making did not turn out as he had hoped, so he crushed it into a lump of clay again and started over. Then the Lord gave me this message: "O Israel, can I not do to you as this potter has done to his clay? As the clay is in the potter's hand, so are you in my hand."
Jeremiah 18:1–6 NLT

Crushed

After my first round of chemotherapy on February 11, 2020, Don wrote me a friendly reminder: Write your own experiences along the way. Write your own story before a liar tells it for you. Utilize Microsoft Word and do not share it with anyone, not even me. Share it with NO ONE. Only you will see the depths. Write your own story so you won't have to defend the truth. This is being written to you as is, DON'T ask me questions. Scripture reminded me that *"the end of a matter is better than its beginning, and patience is better than pride"* (Ecclesiastes 7:8 NIV).

On February 25, 2020, I was taken to bay #11. When the nurses pre-medicated me with the required medicines before beginning my chemo, I was feeling confident and ready.

Now faith is the substance of things hoped for, the evidence of things not seen.
Hebrews 11:1

Minutes into the second round of chemo I had a reaction to the medication. I felt like I was suffocating, and I panicked, grabbed Don's arm and said, "I feel nauseous. I can't breathe. I'm calling the doctor." I pressed the assistance button nonstop.

"Don't panic," Don said.

The doctors rushed to my bay. As they hooked me up to an oxygen tank, all I could say was, "Jesus, Jesus, Jesus."

"On a scale of one to ten, what's your pain level?" the doctor asked. With my legs trembling and lower abdominal pain increasing, I felt fire rising on my insides, intensifying the pain in my lower extremities. I said, "Six."

The doctor asked me again, "What is your pain level on a scale of one to ten?"

Suddenly I began crying, and while I continued trembling and feeling the burn, I felt relief and the Holy Spirit revealing to me that I was being healed from the inside, and from all other medical prognoses I had received before my cancer diagnosis. I said, "Four." Then, "He is healing me right now." As I declared I was being healed in Jesus's name, the pain dissipated.

I remained in the bay for three hours. After I took a nap, the doctor tried to administer the chemo one more time, but the same sensation returned after one minute. I couldn't complete the treatment. I was never going to take Taxol again and was officially done with that part of treatment.

Don said, "You are calling on Jesus, but He is calling on you!" I meditated and remembered, the day before, how the father of one of my students at SEU told me to read 1 Peter 4 with my husband. It was at that moment I read this passage and knew He was teaching me something new.

Beloved, do not be surprised at the fiery trial when it comes upon you to test you, as though something strange were happening to you. But rejoice insofar as you share Christ's sufferings, that you may also rejoice and be glad when his glory is revealed. If you are insulted for the name of Christ, you are blessed, because the Spirit of glory and of God rests upon you. But let none of you suffer as a murderer or a thief or an evildoer or as a meddler. Yet if anyone suffers as a Christian, let him not be ashamed, but let him glorify God in that name. For it is time for judgment to begin at the household of God; and if it begins with us, what will be the outcome for those who do not obey the gospel of God? And "If the righteous is scarcely saved, what will become of the ungodly and the sinner?" Therefore let those who suffer according to God's will entrust their souls to a faithful Creator while doing good."
1 Peter 4:12–19 ESV

The doctor assured me that she would put up a fight for my life the moment I reacted to the medication. I was not done in this life, and the Lord spared my life with his love and supernatural power. The word from God at the beginning, after my first treatment confirmed by my doctor the morning of treatment number two, was enough evidence that this process was all in God's hands and no man would change that.

Upon returning home that afternoon, I was relieved to know that I would be receiving a new treatment. I had three weeks to prepare. I was able to work out a plan with my supervisors to work from home. At this point, COVID-19 was ramping up and the news was beginning to surface at the university. We were not quarantined or told to remain home yet, but the Lord provided a way and my employer was flexible, providing the resources for me to work from home.

The bottom line was that I needed to stop my own agenda and connect with the Lord. How would I be able to do this with chemo, working full-time, a husband, and a son? It was as easy as realizing it was not by my might or by my own power but by God's Spirit. I was reluctant to take on anything I didn't have to, and it would be all or nothing for the sake of obedience. Danilo learned to say, "Obedience is greater than sacrifice," and it was a healthy reminder.

Letting go of control was one of the hardest tests I had to face as it revealed what I was always afraid of—letting go of fear. God sets us up to pass the test, and I was learning that each level of testing was preparing me for a greater measure of faith. The only way to combat the fiery darts of fear is through faith.

Above all, taking the shield of faith with which you will be able to quench all the fiery darts of the wicked one.

Ephesians 6:16

In *Crushing*, T. D. Jakes says, "Now more than ever, it's crucial that we begin seeing that the plans we have imagined for our lives cannot compare to God's strategy for fulfilling our divine purpose." Our plans do not compare to the Master's strategy. Transformation is beyond what we can accomplish and achieve in life.

Crushing is part of the process for maturation. Crushing reveals there is more to our life than what we had planned and hoped for. Without lingering on how that makes us feel, the process takes us through a new stage of faith, growth, and development, which leaves us prepared for a new level of understanding that our past could never reveal.

The truth about my cancer process was not about being afraid of the possibility of dying; instead, it was about faith in the birth of a new life full of new hope, dreams, and purpose. Although I once said I would never take chemotherapy if I was ever diagnosed with cancer, I quickly accepted the medical advice when I knew that my alternatives for the military were slim to none without the full process being complete. I went through my journals and prayers, sermon notes and sticky note reminders as I wrote my story, and the Word of God is truth in my life. The scripture John wrote resonated with me, "He must increase, but I must decrease." John 3:30, NLT.

Back on October 13, 2019, Bishop Ruddy Gracia peached a sermon titled "It Was Not a Plan for Death But for Life." Genesis 50:20–21 says, "'You intended to harm me, but God intended it all for good. He brought me to this position so I could save the lives of many people. No, don't be afraid. I will continue to take care of you and your children.' So, he reassured them by speaking kindly to them" (NLT). Joseph dreamed to bless others according to God's purpose. God advances us to bless others. This is why He fills us with rivers, not lagoons. The Lord made Joseph's dreams, and the Enemy was determined to stop that blessing.

But Jesus has come to give us abundant life, as we learn in John 10:10. Joseph's brothers were filled with hatred, but Joseph rose out of a prison. When Satan opened the plan of death, God opened the door for the plan of life. Bishop Gracia ended his sermon with a reminder to us that God has a plan and the first thing you will give to your son is faith. In other words, my future generation was my biggest reason for preparing in faith for what was to come.

That is what the Scriptures mean when they say, "No eye has seen, no ear has heard,
and no mind has imagined what God has prepared for those who love him."
1 Corinthians 2:9 NLT

As I recorded the main points of this sermon, I received the affirmation to move forward in faith and trust that I was moving along with God's perfect plan. He predestined us for glory. It is coming in His redemption—the redemption that no other prince of this generation has ever known but by the crucifixion (death and apparent defeat) of Jesus then raised from death. Today we live because He died and rose again.

When a problem appears, the provision is already present. Rejoice in the midst of the test. The Enemy does not think to attack you; he just attacks. When something attacks you, God opens the door to life. In Daniel 3, Shadrach, Meshach, and Abednego were men of God sold to a purpose. They refused to obey the law to bow to the altar of Nebuchadnezzar's god.

Our weapons are not carnal. We dictate what happens in the nations by the Spirit. We have the anointing. Jehovah wins this battle. Death will give way to life. There is light because there would be darkness. There would be no light without darkness. In conclusion, the devil has no wisdom.

When you see a death plan:

- Believe it will result in a blessing and will bring life to many. Remember the story of Lazarus in John 12:19.
- Never assume that the Enemy is in control (Genesis 45:5).
- God used the Enemy to lead Joshua to the throne. God has a plan.
- Focus on the eternal plan. Troubles are momentary. They are all light. Eternal weight of glory (2 Corinthians 4:16–18).
- Wait for the breakthrough (Micah 19:8).
- The Lord will be my light (Job 19:5).
- The son of God will be glorified (John 12:23)

At the end of listening to this sermon, I felt ready to move forward with the plans set in place. I was confident that my next battle would break me, form me, shape me, transform me, and reveal God's glory.

The thought of having to go through chemotherapy was not frightening the night before, but it was the first time I'd felt the most comfort I cried and Don held me, saying, "It's going to be okay." Instantly, I knew God was in control and He had already blessed me with everything I needed to get through this chapter. I was looking forward to the outcome as I felt peace with the diagnosis and my trust in the Lord. Good things take time to develop. I began to understand this was a growing process I'd never endured, and I was joyful to accept a new challenge.

"I am the true vine, and my Father is the gardener. He cuts off every branch in me that bears no fruit, while every branch that does not bear fruit. He prunes so that it will be even more fruitful. You are already clean because of the word I have spoken to you. Remain in me, as I also remain in you. No branch can bear fruit by itself; it must remain in the vine. Neither can you bear fruit unless you remain in me."

John 15:1–4 NIV

One of my cousins asked me, "Why do you think you need to go through chemotherapy?" I was not one hundred percent convinced about anything the doctors were telling me. But "the latent potential within us can only be realized under horizontal pressure for vertical purposes." In other words, the cross.

Little did I know that it would take a medicine as strong as death to fight cancer, but it took faith in Christ to gain life. As we learn in Luke 2:52, how Jesus grew in stature and in favor, with God and with men, bearing fruits, so we realize He grew by going through the trials, difficulties, and processes we would have to endure.

God is not a man, so he does not lie.
He is not human, so he does not change his mind.
Has he ever spoken and failed to act?
Has he ever promised and not carried it through?
Numbers 23:19 NLT

Botija

While livestreaming Wednesday night church service, I heard Bishop Ruddy Gracia say "like *botija de barro*." I googled *botija* de barro and discovered that a *botija* is not only the name of one of the characters from my favorite tv Spanish shows *Chespirito* and *El Chavo del Ocho*. Botija is also a large round clay pot that looks exactly the way I was described as a baby, fat. It was that moment when the Holy Spirit brought me to "and the vessel that he made of clay was marred in the hand of the potter; so he made it again into another vessel, as it seemed good to the potter to make" (Jeremiah 1:4 NIV).

I have often heard Yesenia Then, and other teachers explain the meaning of names particularly given to individuals in the Bible depicting their destiny or perhaps a new name given when re-routed along the way. For example, the stories of Abram changed to Abraham, Jacob to Israel, and Saul to Paul. I recognize it is important for me to note that my name may have been given to me without a logical understanding but how God will use this valuable lesson to teach me that everything in my life has meaning is imperative for me to share with you.

Botija was a fictional character played by actor from Mexico Dr. Edgar

Vivar who also played "Señor or Barriga," and his son, "Ñoño," and resigned from his roles on the tv series realizing they were no longer appropriate due to losing 165 pounds on his weight loss journey. Botija was also known as a potbellied earthenware jug or jar used to transport kerosene from Spain to the Caribbean and used to hide money underground. They were buried to prevent humidity from reaching the floor. Later, botijas were dug up and considered a Caribbean musical instrument of the aerophone that Cubans would play in their son of the 19th century also known for having its roots in the Puerto Rican salsa. Also, noteworthy, the name given to a barrio municipality of Orocovis, Puerto Rico.

My nickname meant more to me than I had ever imagined, and it only took digging a little deeper, with the help from the Holy Spirit, rather than my family's explanations.

As I became flooded with peace from the revelation I was receiving, suddenly I had something to work with and the *botija* which had been shattered into pieces meant more to God than I could ever fathom. I acknowledge my life has been full of blessings beyond measure, but I lacked an experience that I could live to tell, a revelation I had yet to receive, and the patience to wait, until the confirmation knocked at my door.

I received several messages from people who were watching my journey via social media. They asked me, "Are you journaling? Are you going to write a book?" Of course, I felt the pulling and His timing was perfect. It was time to experience the fullness of God's grace and the moment this story would be written, in my weakness, and in my time of total dependence on my Father in heaven.

But he said to me, "My grace is sufficient for you, for my power is made perfect in weakness." Therefore, I will boast all the more gladly about my weaknesses, so that Christ's power may rest on me.
2 Corinthians 12:9 NIV

I wanted to tell my family. I wanted to celebrate the journey of writing a book with them. But God planted it in my heart to write. In a matter of weeks before my last treatment in chemotherapy, my family endured the loss of my *abuelo* and heaven's gain. I promised him, before he passed, that I would complete that thing—my dream to go into the Air Force. The truth about my dream to go into the military was in the realization of other matters God wanted to teach me.

The day I began the compilation of records, journals, prayers, and pieces to my story, marked one year from the day I had prayed asking God if it was okay to write about my life, June 12, 2020. I wanted to tell my story, and *Abuelo's* passing left me with courage to rise up and write it. Though I would have never wanted him to know, while he lived, all that had taken place in my past, I would never want to retain what God did regardless of everything in hopes that it could be of encouragement to others who desire a breakthrough healing.

In the past I had become fearful of sharing my thoughts, plans, ideas, and dreams. I'd been inflexible prior to my process of healing. When Don and I got together in 2015, I remember telling him that I no longer desired to dream, I just wanted to do. What I meant was, I did not know how to dream, especially without vision. Like many of you, I felt muzzled because of fear, my vision was clouded by what I couldn't control, and I focused on what people would say, do, or think.

This might resonate with many of you as we faced our reality with a global pandemic in 2020. But Bishop Gracia always mentions that to see the supernatural, it is necessary to stop focusing on the natural. For years I had been crippled spiritually and unable to convey who I truly am. I became someone God never intended for me to be, until He released me from my own pit of despair and required of me to do what He created me to do within the four walls of my prison called breast cancer.

Do you recall the story of Joseph, and what happened when he shared his God-given dreams with his brothers? Have you ever related to passages that speak to you about the life you have known in one way or another? For me, it would be the case with Joseph from Genesis 37, the Samaritan woman from John 4, and the lepers in 2 Kings 7. Why do I tell you this? Because God chose to bless these people to go and tell, to fulfill His Word.

Why did I fight all my life? I wanted to tell my story. It was finally time, even though the Enemy struck me with every reason to give up. This process taught me to keep moving. Even when things seemed to come crashing down, moving would produce breakthroughs of deliverance, healing, and restoration. I made a choice. I decided to tell. Though I was not going to die, I would die if I didn't try. Like the four lepers from 2 Kings 7, I was determined to move and be liberated once and for all.

Every time in the past, when I ran to tell my parents about something good, just when I thought I would be celebrated by them, my dad would say, "Don't tell anyone that." But those words remind me of the story of Esther and her uncle Mordecai. Dad was right for telling me to keep certain things to myself at an early stage in my life, but the time would come where keeping quiet could cost the life of many seeking deliverance. On one occasion Mordecai would ask her to remain silent, and on another he was warning her that even she would lose her life if the enemy discovered their nationality, but she would have to rise up and speak even if it could cost her life.

Esther had not told anyone of her nationality and family background, because Mordecai had directed her not to do so. Every day Mordecai would take a walk near the courtyard of the harem to find out about Esther and what was happening to her.
Esther 2:10 NLT

When Haman saw that Mordecai would not bow down or show him respect, he was filled with rage. He had learned of Mordecai's nationality, so he decided it was not enough to lay hands on Mordecai alone. Instead, he looked for a way to destroy all the Jews throughout the entire empire of Xerxes.
Esther 3:5–7 NLT

Mordecai sent this reply to Esther: 'Don't think for a moment that because you're in the palace you will escape when all other Jews are killed. If you keep quiet at a time like this, deliverance and relief for the Jews will arise from some other place, but you and your relatives will die. Who knows if perhaps you were made queen for just

such a time as this?" Then Esther sent this reply to Mordecai: "Go and gather together
all the Jews of Susa and fast for me. Do not eat or drink for
three days, night or day. My maids and I will do the same. And then, though it is
against the law, I will go in to see the king. If I must die, I must die." So Mordecai
went away and did everything as Esther had ordered him.
Esther 3:7–16 NLT

As if I was supposed to protect myself from something. I even had friends look at me with disdain at times when I spoke up with the truth, and say, "I can't believe you would say that," referring to my remarks about things I could see were clearly wrong.

I thank God for all the names I was given. I thank God for the pointers; they each set me up for the right direction in one way or another. Especially for such time as this as we learn from the book of Esther. All the God-given beauty she bore was not in vain when she discovered her purpose in this world, a greater purpose she understood, which would be useful to deliver her people out of danger.

In my case, I learned, the gifts, God deposited into me as a child would be useful one day, and regardless of the outward appearance vanishing with a process, the inward me was being renewed day by day in faith, hope, and joy. I desired nothing less than to be chosen and used to advance the kingdom of heaven in a world corrupted and consumed by sin, deceit, and suffering.

The voices I once heard helped me see the very essence of who I truly can be and where I ought to use those gifts. Rather than wasting those gifts on the mundane affairs of this world, it was time to be trained up and pour those gifts into the assignment God placed into this Botija, a vessel. After all, what more was I going to lose, my reputation, my money, my vanity, myself? What good would it be now to keep what the Lord has done in my life all to myself?

Scribe

By the end of my chemotherapy treatment, God restored all my dreams, but I was put to a challenge. I was set up when speaking on it once again. When I shared the good news with my brother, about my book and my excitement about my conversation with my publisher, he said, "Don't tell me anymore, because you know the devil is listening." Not only was I attempting to mind my own business about everyone's affairs in my family, but I was challenged to filter things I did not want to hear.

I knew I was not going to win a spiritual fight in the flesh. I would see to it that I pray and move forward at peace with the conviction from the Holy Spirit. I realized that my language was uncommon to my family because of my faith. I had to be broken free from pride and self-righteousness. I knew God hates both of those among the six things He hates according to Proverbs 6:16–19. It was the end of my rope of spiritual suicide, and I was no longer going to give thought to what it could be like if everyone in my family could be on the same page. Though my phone did not ring for three weeks after that moment, I was at peace with the outcome as the Holy Spirit gave me His word.

'Don't imagine that I came to bring peace to the earth! I came not to bring peace, but a sword.
'I have come to set a man against his father,
a daughter against her mother,
and a daughter-in-law against her mother-in-law.
Your enemies will be right in your own household!'
If you love your father or mother more than you love me, you are not worthy of being mine; or if you love your son or daughter more than me, you are not worthy of being mine. If you refuse to take up your cross and follow me, you are not worthy of being mine."
Matthew 10:34–38 NLT

I prayed and asked God to protect my heart. I did not want to go back to where He had rescued me from. It was at that moment I would no longer speak with my family regarding my Father's affairs and I would choose to move forward knowing that it would be a narrow path. I could relate to Job, who became estranged from my family and acquaintances. That was the beginning of a heavenly download of memories, from my childhood, from my teenage years, into my adult years, through the moments of my treatment from which I would become the scribe for the completion of my first book.

Oh, that my words could be recorded.
Oh, that they could be inscribed on a monument,
carved with an iron chisel and filled with lead,
engraved forever in the rock.
But as for me, I know that my Redeemer lives,
and he will stand upon the earth at last.
And after my body has decayed,
yet in my body I will see God!
I will see him for myself.
Yes, I will see him with my own eyes.
I am overwhelmed at the thought!
Job 19:23–27 NIV

I want you to know that regardless if you have felt afraid, unsupported, ashamed, ridiculed, mocked, outcast, or rejected the way the chapters of this book reflect all the natural and satanic tactics we experience on this earthly life, if you are reading this, God has chosen you. He has called you, and it is without hesitation that I remind you what the apostle Paul wrote: "God chose the lowly things of this world and the despised things—and the things that are not—to nullify the things that are" (1 Corinthians 1:28 NLT).

The other aspect of this painful separation came with ample learning curves that I reflected on day after day on the lanai at our house in Lakeland. I was grateful for God's pruning. Though incredibly challenging at times, I got up and talked a lot with the Lord about my ways. The memories and the revelations came to me, and I would have to revisit feelings I had once let go of. These memories and feelings brought on conversations with Don and I where I would receive sound advice that was hard to chew and swallow. Humility was knocking at my door and pleading for me to say, "Please enter."

I was afraid of letting my guard down, but what God was showing me came with grace. He permitted my family to move away so He could develop me and reveal a better version. I will never tell anyone to unconcern themselves with what people say or think. In any capacity the Lord wills to place us in, it is important to consider our testimony and the way we exemplify our creator.

Character is developed in the most crushing times of our life, and in many ways, it is necessary to depart from the distractions and noise, while many of us are not always graced with this opportunity. I began to thank God increasingly for the quarantine and for the time I would spend at home. Bishop T. D. Jakes wrote, "For if people get too close to us during the process of casting off everything we have failed to release over the years, those same people can easily be rendered spiritually unconscious, never wanting to have anything to do with us or the Vintner we wish to emulate."

On May 23, 2020, I was so thankful for these words. I knew that a time would come of supreme rest in the Lord, and separation from all that was keeping me busy in my own mind. I wanted to practice caution in my communication with others. It was challenging. Many people were asking me, "How do you feel today?" I believe I was getting text messages daily, and I would reply, "Praise God, all is well.

Warrior

I confess, I used to be like a loose cannon when I heard things that provoked me to anger. But the Bible teaches us to "be wise as serpents and harmless as doves" (Matthew 10:16). Here is a secret: when you have been delivered from something, you do not have to worry about going there again as long as you remain in complete devotion to God, in spirit and in truth.

"I am the Lord your God, who rescued you from the land of Egypt, the place of your slavery." Exodus 20:2 NLT

My constant battle with words, deception, and anger ended when I was put to the test during my cycles of chemo treatment and juggling multiple interpersonal relationships. My family and friends kept calling me *Guerrera* (warrior), but the warrior was in training for the battle. It was time to resist the temptation in the wilderness. A warrior woman arose. No longer was the Enemy going to have a place in my house, but when he showed up, it was his last time.

For the first six months of 2020, my virtual group was praying and interceding without ceasing for breakthroughs in our family, for unity, for deliverance, and for healing as we faced some of the most vicious trials of affliction from addictions to cancer. The moment we believed victory was at hand, we counted to the very last second to receive Normarie back with open arms from her process.

I share this with you because from our young years living in Germany to the present moment this story is being written, we have come to know that nothing can separate us from God's love, and we declared this year that we would live to tell our stories.

Can anything ever separate us from Christ's love? Does it mean he no longer loves us if we have trouble or calamity, or are persecuted, or hungry, or destitute, or in danger, or threatened with death? (As the Scriptures say, "For your sake we are killed every day; we are being slaughtered like sheep.") No, despite all these things, overwhelming victory is ours through Christ, who loved us. And I am convinced that nothing can ever separate us from God's love. Neither death nor life, neither angels nor demons, neither our fears for today nor our worries about tomorrow—not even the powers of hell can separate us from God's love. No power in the sky above or in the earth below—indeed, nothing in all creation will ever be able to separate us from the love of God that is revealed in Christ Jesus our Lord.
Romans 8:35–39 NLT

One of my favorite passages of scripture, one I have often heard Yesenia Then preach from, resonated when mentioned during one of the Redoma 2020 segments. It would help me understand how to overcome the enemy when he tried to set foot in my territory. In Judges 4:17–24, we find a story of a woman relatable to the Word from Genesis 3:15 and Judges 4:14, as she received the victory when the enemy set foot in her house. She was wise, she was clever, she was decisive, she was kind, but she nailed it. Her name is Jael. She was the woman Deborah prophesied about in Judges 4. But the interesting fact about Jael is that she did not know she would rise up to be a warrior, but she proved to be effective.

Meanwhile, Sisera ran to the tent of Jael, the wife of Heber the Kenite, because Heber's family was on friendly terms with King Jabin of Hazor. Jael went out to meet Sisera and said to him, "Come into my tent, sir. Come in. Don't be afraid." So he went into her tent, and she covered him with a blanket. "Please give me some water," he said. "I'm thirsty." So she gave him some milk from a leather bag and covered him again. "Stand at the door of the tent," he told her. "If anybody comes and asks you if there is anyone here, say no." But when Sisera fell asleep from exhaustion, Jael quietly crept up to him with a hammer and tent peg in her hand. Then she drove the tent peg through his temple and into the ground, and so he died. When Barak came looking for Sisera, Jael went out to meet him. She said, "Come, and I will show you the man you are looking for." So he followed her into the tent and found Sisera lying there dead, with the tent peg through his temple. So on that day Israel saw God defeat Jabin, the Canaanite king. And from that time on Israel became stronger and stronger against King Jabin until they finally destroyed him.
Judges 4:14–23 NLT"

Restored

His unconditional love, mercy, and grace restored my life. It came from a source I had never truly known before, an incomprehensible faith that no matter how much appeared to be a loss, was restored by just reaching and grabbing the border of his mantle. I experienced shalom, (peace), nothing missing, nothing broken.

I can testify that He showed me nothing was lost unless for a better purpose.

The thousands of dollars lost at the second attempt to purchase a house would be overturned for His glory. A sister in Christ, messaged me at the peak of my chemo side effects on Friday, June 5, 2020, telling me that she had been following my journey. Meanwhile, my sister Yvette was keeping me in the loop with her military orders and training for the Air Force, and Normarie was conquering other matters of life and death that would become her living testimony. All was not lost, and I praise God for the woman who stepped in our favor to protect our investment, and later shared with me she had become a follower of Jesus Christ. Although Don and I never purchased the second house in Palm Beach and money was lost, a soul was reached, it was her.

For this reason, I exhort you to choose wisely when asking something from God. Be careful not to tell Him what to do as you pray and be careful to not call a blessing from God a curse, as my husband would always tell me. I had to choose between closeness with my family, everything I had once known, and my personal desires, over the reality of my constant separation from everything and complete dependence on my Father. He would show me what was happening behind the scenes, and all I was doing was praying and resting in Him.

See that no one pays back evil for evil, but always try to do good to each other and to all people. Always be joyful. Never stop praying. Be thankful in all circumstances, for this is God's will for you who belong to Christ Jesus. Do not stifle the Holy Spirit. Do not scoff at prophecies, but test everything that is said. Hold on to what is good. Stay away from every kind of evil.
1 Thessalonians 5:15–21 NLT

By the end of my last treatment, my body experienced total depletion of energy and stamina, with extreme fatigue and anemia. It goes without saying, I did not get to practice normalcy at home with Danilo, Don, or work as it pertained to activities with the same intensity as before going through cancer treatment, but God. The Holy Spirit revealed to me God's constant protection over my house, my marriage, and my finances, and how constant attacks that the Enemy tried to bring—death, destruction, and division to my family could not prevail. The Holy Spirit revealed how cancer and chemotherapy, my grandfather's passing, my friend's family members passing on due to COVID-19, slander that came to my phone about my character and about my church did not prosper. No weapon against me prospered.

> *But the Lord says,*
> *"The captives of warriors will be released,*
> *and the plunder of tyrants will be retrieved.*
> *For I will fight those who fight you,*
> *and I will save your children."*
> *Isaiah 49:50 NLT*

My battle for life was at stake as God removed the veil from my eyes and revealed how the Enemy got awfully close to me, but I would not be taken out. What he intended for harm God turned for good. I received phone calls from loved ones, friends, and people I esteem, testifying of what God was doing, and of family, friends, and their families surviving COVID-19, overcoming addictions, and getting saved by grace. To God be the glory. Though crushing, separation, isolation was evident, I felt an immense amount of peace anticipating my surgery, which was next on the calendar.

Survivor

The days before my right partial radical mastectomy, I was faced with my biggest obstacle: overcoming my fear. My faith was not in the process I needed to endure but in Christ who would go through it with me. Leaning on Don for more insight and praying for peace were my only hope. Everyone else waited for me to call them and tell them the mass had disappeared and I would not be undergoing surgery. Ideally, that would have been grand. Days leading up to surgery, we even heard several testimonies of women who had suffered from breast cancer, survived without chemotherapy or surgery, and even had a baby.

On July 13, 2020, I was listening to Yesenia Then on YouTube preaching about Peter and his faith, by the word that was given, she said, "It's not about what the doctors said. I told you that by this time next year you would be holding a child referring to the word from 2 Kings 4 once again. It was not what they said. Suddenly, as she continued in her sermon, the Holy Spirit told her to speak these words:

Right now, I see a woman who has cancer sitting in her house, I see you sitting on your sofa. You lost all your hair because you had chemotherapy. I see you with a scarf on your head, and you felt very sad, but the Lord says, "because I have interrupted this message, you have your head down and you are shaking your head asking, 'Lord, is this me?' Yes, this is to you. It's to you, woman, who was attacked by the spirit of cancer. Receive liberation, receive healing, because you will rise out of this with a testimony that will sweep your house. Not because of what the doctor said, but what my Word says. You will testify and church get ready because I am going to bring the testimony here. What God has been doing here via transmissions, we have been modest. But this testimony, I can feel right now, how the fire of the Holy Spirit touches all your body and I will receive this testimony. Woman, you are free. Woman, you are healed. Woman, you are free and healed in the name of Jesus of Nazareth.'"

I fell to my knees crying out, and Don asked me, "Are you okay?" He normally would not be seated next to me when I was watching my services on the TV, but this time it was hilarious, because I was crying and laughing at once, and he said, "I can't tell if you are crying or laughing."
I told him what Yesenia had said in Spanish and he agreed with me to request one more scan at the hospital. Of course, I wanted to believe that I was free from surgery as well. But not exactly! I went to my doctor on the following Monday and scheduled an MRI Friday before my surgery. The clock was ticking. I was content with my results. Chemotherapy had reduced the mass significantly.

But the doctor told me I was going to complete the process because it was necessary. They knew my story from when I walked in, January 2020. For me to receive a clearance to go into the USAF, I would need to complete treatment. This reminds me of the lessons I have heard Yesenia teach related to Gilgal—the place of many who are called and chosen do not want to go through. It hurts to be cut. But she also said on many of her segments, *"Sin atajos"* (English translation "without shortcuts"). I had peace. Don told me on our drive home, "I knew already." I just needed to realize it for myself, the best was yet to come. He always told me, "Enjoy the process."

I learned a great lesson taking my time with Bishop T. D. Jakes' *Crushing*, "In our rush to escape the pain, messiness, and brokenness of our lives, however, we often miss our opportunities for growth. Mired in the muck of our misguided mindsets, we miss what God may be doing in the midst of this dirty place. With a heave, a strain, a shove, a stretch, and a charge upward, you fight to leave the place you were planted, because surely you believe that God has to have something better for you than where you've come from and where you go."

God's timing, His strategies, and presence never left me. Amid COVID-19, the hospital maintained a no-visitation policy. For the duration of my appointments, treatments, and consultations between March 2020 through present day, Don and Danilo had to remain in the vehicle waiting for me without an opportunity to be next to me. The moment I panicked during my second chemotherapy treatment, I was being prepared for the biggest step of faith I would have ever taken, general anesthesia for six hours and waking up to missing my right breast. Surely this would not be the worse battle I have yet to conquer, but it was a victorious one.

He said, "I came naked from my mother's womb,
and I will be naked when I leave.
The Lord gave me what I had,
and the Lord has taken it away.
Praise the name of the Lord!"
In all of this, Job did not sin by blaming God.
Job 1:21–22 NLT

In September 2020, when I got a series of phone calls from friends and family about their recovery from COVID-19 after their attempt to visit me, I fell to my knees in total surrender unto God. I realized the Enemy tried to cut my life short, but that God's sovereignty prevails. I learned quickly that He did not have to explain the plans He had for me or the method He would use. I needed to receive and understand the process. Trusting Him with my entire life was vital to discover the fear I was able to overcome in Him.

Refraining from too many phone calls, filtering my thoughts, and focusing on specific instructions from the Holy Spirit may be the most difficult thing I have ever done, but there is blessing in obedience. This may have been the same thing my mom was attempting to teach me when she cut off my text-messaging capability in college. But denying visitation from loved ones was tough, until I finally saw what God was showing me.

His infinite love and protection for His interest weighed more than my own effort. He was waiting on me to trust Him. With that I accepted the process in full confidence that He was working out affairs of this world in ways man could never fathom. Proven fact, during this pandemic, no man was able to come up with a more effective or efficient way to save my family from the destruction of COVID-19 and cancer, but God.

Redoma 2020 had been postponed until September 2020 and themed, "Her Story." Some of the greatest moments of laughter, joy, love, peace, and reflection came during my process of chemotherapy followed by the unexpected and divine miracle of celebrating Redoma with my cousin Normarie and Titi Carmen for their first time. Thousands of women came from South Florida, Nevada, Texas, and Washington, D.C., among other cities.

It was the first time in seven months that our speakers had stepped on a platform to minister the Word of God and the mold of fear was broken. The presence of the Holy Spirit consumed the atmosphere in a glorious way as Prophetess Cindy Jacobs, Omayra Font, Vanessa Gracia Cruz, Bishop Ruddy Gracia, Maryam Delgado, and Paula Maria Arrazola brought a fresh word to our spirit.

I shall not die, but live, and declare the works of the Lord.
Psalms 118:17 KJV

My Prayer Journal: November 2, 2020

"Should we accept only good things from the hand of God and never anything bad?" So
in all this, Job said nothing wrong." Job 2:10 NLT

On October 18, 2019, Breast Cancer Awareness Month, a mass was discovered in my right breast. On November 18, 2019, an ultrasound detected multiple dark spots and lymph nodes confirming it was imperative that I get a biopsy. On December 28, 2019, I began my journey to the Moffitt Cancer Institute in Tampa, Florida. On January 9, 2020, after a second ultrasound, three biopsies and a mammogram, a Pet Scan, CT Scan, an additional 3 biopsies combined with another mammogram, two MRIs and a Bone Scan, sixty-three visits later, three COVID-screenings, and the onset of early menopause at 34 years of age, we have reached day number 380. The Lord told me, "When you go through deep waters, I will be with you. When you go through rivers of difficulty, you will not drown. When you walk through the fire of oppression, you will not be burned up; the flames will not consume you." Isaiah 43:2 NLT

Today we celebrate the VICTORY, of completing fifteen rounds of Neoadjuvant Chemotherapy (one Taxol, nine Abraxane, four Adriamycin), Radical Partial Mastectomy of my right breast, and the removal of sixteen lymph nodes (mass spanning from twelve cm reduced to four cm to total removal, and ten of sixteen lymph nodes cancerous, with three remaining positive and removed), resulting in final diagnosis "Stage three-c Breast Cancer," followed by thirty rounds of radiation to the right chest wall and lymph node axilla. The first three phases of my treatment plan have finished, and I will be entering phase four with hormonal chemotherapy (Zoladex and Anastrozole) for a duration of ten years preventing and canceling the possibility of a repeated case. Let's just call that an injection of faith in Jesus' name.

I have fought the good fight, I have finished the race, and I have remained faithful. And now the prize awaits me—the crown of righteousness, which the Lord, the righteous Judge, will give me on the day of his return. And the prize is not just for me but for all who eagerly look forward to his appearance. 2 Timothy 4:7-8

CHAPTER SEVENTEEN

An Invitation

And there is no one who calls on Your name,
Who stirs himself up to take hold of You;
For You have hidden Your face from us,
And have consumed us because of our iniquities.
But now, O Lord,
You are our Father;
We are the clay, and You our potter;
And all we are the work of Your hand.
Do not be furious, O Lord,
Nor remember iniquity forever;
Indeed, please look—we all are Your people!
Isaiah 64:7–9

Purpose-Driven

We tend to think He will never restore us, bring us back to our original form, or use us for His purpose because of our failed attempts and constant self-seeking plans that provoke us to discouragement and frustration. It takes courage to let go and trust by faith, prayer, and obedience, knowing that we will fulfill what He purposed for us from the beginning and we will give Him the glory and praise for the triumphant victory.

But Jesus said to him, "No one, having put his hand to the plow, and looking back, is fit for the kingdom of God." Luke 9:62 As I researched Botija and clay became the theme in this process, I discovered the Enemy's number one purpose was to mark my life with rejection, abandonment, resentment, fear, and insecurities. The Enemy's objective has always been to spew lies into the life of those with divine purpose. His second tactic is religious oppression, as he wins when we fall into a spiritual mold of victimization, condemnation, and self-loathing before God.

The explanation of how to transform mud into pottery may signify a major leap forward for prehistoric cultures, and until the development of metal cooking pots, ceramic pottery was the pinnacle of cooking technology. But clay pots are lighter than soapstone and easier to transport. They also heat up faster than stone vessels and can be made in much larger sizes than stone vessels. They can be big enough to feed a village from one pot.

My healing process led me to seek and find through Scripture who God says I am and what I can learn from this journey so that I could share it with you. The process of forming the clay into a pot for use reminded me of the process God showed Jeremiah from his calling, to his visit to the potter's house, to his purpose as a prophet to the nations. But first Jeremiah had to change his mind. He said to the Lord, "Ah, Lord God! Behold, I cannot speak, for I am a youth" (Jeremiah 1:6).

When Elisha the man of God spoke to the Shunamite, in 2 Kings 4:14–15, that by this time next year she would embrace a son, she told Elisha, "No, my lord. Man of God, do not lie to your maidservant!" In both texts, I realized, it was not the Word of God that was void of truth but the void of faith that keeps us from believing God's promises when we do not understand them. Rather than asking God why we go through a process, we need to trust His promises which are yes and amen and believe that He that has begun a good work in us will finish it.

I discovered more about the places that I had been allowed to travel through.

But more unique to me, the places this Botija was allowed to be transported to. I'd been like that old rugged pot that has been saturated and you never want to get rid of because "you never know," what it can be used for. But for His use, I would also have to pass through those areas for spiritual circumcision, cleansing, revelation and eventually the supernatural. Only then would I know in whom I put all my faith in, Christ. I had come full circle and realized I had lived a life without understanding. It was in that moment, for the first time, I asked God for the truth.

My son, if you accept my words and store up my commands within you, turning your ear to wisdom and applying your heart to understanding."
Proverbs 2:2 NLT

God hears us. I admitted that I had been short-sighted and always planned my own steps. It was time to see beyond self, beyond my own eyes, and to see with insight, the one He would give. As the Word says in Proverbs 16:9, "We can make our plans, but the Lord determines our steps." (NLT)

Each Scripture and passage I have included in my testimony served as truth in ways I had never experienced when my focus was on what I could see and control. It was no longer about being in the city, with the job, at the church building, and surrounded by the people of my liking, with the perfect academic plan, and the career goals I had set out for myself where I could experience a true encounter with Jesus. Like the woman at the well, He came for me and showed me everything I had done. This was the revelation I received when I sat on the lanai at my house in Lakeland during one of my quarantine days. No matter what, He had chosen this moment to show me, through reckoning everything from the past, this would be about true worship and surrendering to God's perfect plan of sharing the gospel. He became my teacher, my friend, my companion, and my source of life now and for all of eternity.

The woman said, "Sir, I see that you are a prophet. Our ancestors worshiped on this
mountain, but you and your people say that it is necessary to worship in Jerusalem."
Jesus said to her, "Believe me, woman, the time is coming when you and your people
will worship the Father neither on this mountain nor in Jerusalem. You and your
people worship what you don't know; we worship what we know because salvation
is from the Jews. But the time is coming—and is here!—when true worshipers will
worship in spirit and truth. The Father looks for those who worship him this way. God
is spirit, and it is necessary to worship God in spirit and truth."
The woman said, "I know that the Messiah is coming, the one who is called the Christ.
When he comes, he will teach everything to us." Jesus said to her, "I Am—the one
who speaks with you." Just then, Jesus' disciples arrived and were shocked that he was
talking with a woman. But no one asked, "What do you want?" or "Why are you
talking with her?" The woman put down her water jar and went into the city. She said
to the people, "Come and see a man who has told me everything I've done! Could this
man be the Christ?"
John 4:19–29 NLT

As people began to call me during my process asking for prayer and just to
talk about the wonders of what God had been doing, I delighted in the Lord as the
Holy Spirit brought to my memory these things because according to the doctors,
I would have brain fog and, though true, it did not stop me from overcoming the
challenges I avoided far too long. I realized that our divine purpose never leaves us
no matter the size of the battle we face in life. It was worth continuing the fight for
life. I have been saved, delivered, raised, healed, restored, and assigned and though I
am but an earthen vessel, made of clay, I carry a story that I must tell everyone until
the end of my days so that God can receive everything that belongs to Him—the
glory, the honor, and the praise.

Though we may endure the process like the shattering and restoration of
a pot of clay, broken in the hands of mankind, in God's hands nothing remains
incomplete or broken. His peace which surpasses all understanding coupled with
our faith and hope is all the assurance we need that He has not lost control of our

life and He has purposed us for greatness in due season. In order to experience the required purification to become sanctified, approved, and useful, we must first know who we are and accept that our story has been written and He is waiting for us to live it to the fullest no matter what unfolds in each chapter. Botija is just the pot of clay who carries the story of a journey in overcoming fear with faith, pain with love, and losses with hope for the next chapter.

Encourager

Dear brothers and sisters, one thing I have learned from this entire journey through the valleys, deserts, and wilderness is this: God encouraged me; therefore, with the courage I took up, I have been called to encourage you. You have read my story and may be wondering, *How does this apply to me? What shall I consider of all of this?*

I tell you, consider Christ as your Savior, and I promise you that He will guide you through your valley, desert, or wilderness. Whether you have doubted what your calling is, where you are, or what surrendering looks like for you, if you are hearing this for the first time, God is calling you. He has invited you to choose Jesus Christ, and you will begin to experience an awakening and a new hope in Him for the faith you need to pursue the calling He has already made upon your life. When you respond with a humble heart and an open mind to what God has promised, you will understand the urgency you have been feeling and you'll waiver no longer with thoughts of fear and condemnation in the name of Jesus.

If you have heard this before and still experience questioning and thoughts of confusion, you'll find a reminder of the commitment you made to God in Christ and will begin to understand the purpose for seeking God for strength and courage rather than looking to yourself for this strength. Remember, you don't need to try to live a sanctified life without word, instruction, and direction from God. In our weakness, He is made stronger. This is your time to discover your divine purpose for following the Word inspired by God through the Holy Spirit. He wants to speak to you. This is a time for us to experience an encounter with the word through the Holy Spirit and begin to understand how fear is against the word God has given to

His children.

This may be your season to experience complete deliverance and liberty as the Holy Spirit flows through you and takes you into new levels of understanding. God is calling you to have faith while facing new challenges and situations He will lead you through as you navigate through your healing journey in your health, marriage, family, or ministry. This is not about logical or rationale actions. Be relentless and adopt this pursuit of life through faith, hope, and love as Christ himself exemplifies for us. This is about the transformative work of the Holy Spirit through continuous seeking, prayer, and fasting. Hebrews 1:1 says, "God, who at various times and in various ways spoke in time past to the fathers by the prophets," still speaks today. Loving this word will build you up for anything tossed in your direction and it will never fail you. Matthew 24:35 reminds us that "Heaven and earth shall pass, but my words shall not pass away." (KJV)

The apostle Paul said, "Not that I have already attained, or am already perfected; but I press on, that I may lay hold of that for which Christ Jesus has also laid hold of me." As we mature along this path together, we develop a new confidence in the Word of God by receiving guidance and wisdom, revelation and light which delivers, heals, and transforms, and restores. I encourage you to try what you have not tried and watch how your confidence and dependence in Him with your faith will never fail you. We have hope. We have victory. We are more than conquerors.

Therefore, we do not lose heart. Even though our outward man is perishing, yet the inward man is being renewed day by day. For our light affliction, which is but for a moment, is working for us a far more exceeding and eternal weight of glory, while we do not look at the things which are seen, but at the things which are not seen. For the things which are seen are temporary, but the things which are not seen are eternal.
2 Corinthians 4:16–18 NIV

CPSIA information can be obtained
at www.ICGtesting.com
Printed in the USA
BVHW081533220321
603169BV00006B/553